Enhancing Self-Esteem:
A Whole Language Approach

Esteem-Building Thematic Units

by
John Gust, M.A.

illustrated by Becky Radtke

Cover design by Teresa Mathis

Copyright © 1994, Good Apple

ISBN No. 0-86653-809-7

Printing No. 98765432

Good Apple
1204 Buchanan St., Box 299
Carthage, IL 62321-0299

Paramount Publishing

Table of Contents

GA1501

Acknowledgements

I would like to give thanks to my teachers who, through their guidance, helped to make this book possible:

To Bill Auksi, principal of Farren Grammar School in Chicago, who truly modeled the meaning of dignity and honor and who helped me with my start in education.

To my fellow teachers of Figueroa St. School in Los Angeles, whom I learned much from: Tonya Stokes, who taught me how to be real and genuine; Shirley Frankl, who suggested that I start on the path towards the eventual manifestation of this book and who taught me how to be gentle; Mark Ledwig, who taught me the meaning of self-acceptance; Gustavo Vasquez, who taught me the meaning of pride; Principal Elzie Evans, who gave me the freedom to test myself and taught me the meaning of patience; and to Belkis Still, who acknowledged my dreams and forever encouraged my efforts, teaching me the meaning of support.

To Jack Canfield, an exemplary teacher, who, through his tremendously powerful seminars and encouragement, taught me the meaning of leadership.

To Sweet Old Bill Brown, who continuously supported my efforts by giving me the gift of listening and taught me how to be both wise and a child at the same time.

And most importantly, to my parents, Richard and Sally Gust, who taught me the meaning of commitment, honesty, and love.

Dedication

As always, to the children.

Introduction

Hey, self-esteem is in! And it's a good thing it is, especially when you understand all that it entails. Self-esteem is more than just thinking you're cool. It means taking responsibility for yourself, acting appropriately, getting along with others, and having a purpose.

How to get more of it is what this book is all about. With concentrated effort people can learn to like themselves more, to have higher self-esteem. Self-esteem can be taught, and as teachers it is our responsibility to teach it. This book was designed to help the teacher to work on self-esteem issues while teaching good solid content at the same time. The objective is to use a whole language approach to develop literature-based thematic units to enhance our students' self-esteem.

This book is about:

- Understanding the true meaning of self-esteem and how important it is that we attend to self-esteem issues within the classroom.

- Describing the whole language philosophy as it applies to enhancing a child's self-esteem.

- Providing five thematic units incorporating a multitude of culturally diverse activities.

- Explaining an effective five-step method for developing literature-based, esteem-building, thematic units.

- Improving our attitudes as teachers to keep us motivated and to make for more effective and humanistic teaching.

After teaching in south-central Los Angeles in gang-infested streets to children who lacked a knowledge of how significant they are, I decided that I wanted to do something about it. I knew that I must find a way to make a difference. And in my efforts I learned that when I took self-esteem-enhancing activities and incorporated them into comprehensive thematic units within a whole language context, my efforts were much more effective. The children were able to understand and develop meaning from the material presented to them.

My hope is that you will be able to make a difference in the lives of your students
and your life by using the materials presented here.
I'm sure you'll find the effort well worth it.

GA1501

Understanding Self-Esteem and Whole Language Teaching

"What we want to see is the child in pursuit of knowledge,
not knowledge in pursuit of the child."
- George Bernard Shaw

What Is Self-Esteem?

In our current competitive school system a student's success or failure is closely associated with ability. Ability is regarded as unchangeable, a condition over which a failing student has no control, and in a competitive system, success or failure becomes strongly associated with high or low ability. This condition promotes learned helplessness and worthlessness. Students, in an effort to move away from feelings of helplessness, then stop trying and drop out of school.

This is why the issue of self-esteem is of major importance in education today. We must understand that as teachers it is our responsibility to enhance the self-esteem of the students in our classroom. Today more than ever, our students' lives depend on it!

However, before we can effectively enhance the self-esteem of children in our classroom, we must first understand the concept of self-esteem. As it's listed in the dictionary, self-esteem is a noun—a person, place, or thing. But, self-esteem is not really a noun; you can't place it in a bread box. Self-esteem is more like a verb—an action. More precisely, self-esteem is a process. A process is a systematic series of actions directed toward some end. Self-esteem is the process of evaluating and judging one's own inner self-descriptions.

In addition, self-esteem is more than just "feeling good." When teaching self-esteem we must realize that we address specific educational needs such as accountability, responsibility, goal setting, problem solving, social skills, self-understanding, and intrinsic motivation. Self-esteem-enhancing practices never have been and never will be just "fun-time" or "filler" activities.

Where Does Self-Esteem Come From?

We develop self-esteem from a variety of sources. Basically, these sources fall into two categories: outer sources and inner sources.

Outer Sources (the five A's)
1. Attention
2. Acceptance
3. Approval
4. Acknowledgement
5. Affection

Inner Sources
1. Value Identification
2. Integrity
3. Personal and Social Responsibility
4. Personal Importance and Significance
5. Purpose
6. Competence

GA1501

Children receive the outer sources of self-esteem from significant others in their lives–friends, family, or teachers. These significant others help children to feel loved, valued, and wanted. As children grow, the way they believe their significant others think and feel about them influences the way they regard, value, and esteem themselves.

The inner sources of self-esteem are acquired from the work the children must experience for themselves. It is our responsibility to provide opportunities and activities for children to attend to these inner sources of self-esteem.

Self-Esteem Building Tools

As teachers, we have special tools that we can use to support and build on the inner and outer sources by which a child acquires self-esteem skills. The building blocks of self-esteem are skills, and the more skillful students are, the more capable they are to cope with life's situations. By using these tools, teachers will be fostering skills of personal and social responsibility, empowering students to enhance their self-esteem and behavioral options.

The activities in this book cover all of the tools listed below:

- Experiential Activities
- Cooperative Activities
- Problem-Solving Activities
- Writing Activities
- Interdisciplinary Activities
- Role Playing

- Affirming Declarations
- Goal Setting
- Movement Exploration
- Cognitive Lessons
- Envisioneering
- Journal Writing

Integrating Self-Esteem-Enhancing Practices and the Whole Language Approach

The whole language philosophy considers the child as the primary determinant of curriculum direction, and this way of thinking strongly supports self-esteem-enhancing practices. By combining a focus on self-esteem enhancement and whole language teaching, teachers can consistently provide experiential activities that invite children to become involved in their learning. When children are involved in their learning, they like what they are doing, they feel good, they stay on task, they generate their own motivation, and they receive positive strokes from others while becoming empowered in the process. Integrating whole language teaching with self-esteem-building practices will promote strong, independent, autonomous learners.

In addition, the whole language classroom requires the teacher to become a model for the children to emulate and a facilitator of student learning. This practice requires the children to take more responsibility for their learning, holding them accountable for their outcomes.

The Whole Language Classroom

The whole language philosophy stresses that communication skills are learned most fully when children participate in a variety of interactive and interpersonal experiences. Whole language instruction takes the student from the whole (the book's theme), to the part (individual skills), back to the whole again (the theme). The whole language philosophy advocates that students are competent and capable learners. The whole language classroom provides students with real-life experiences by which to develop and obtain new language.

The whole language philosophy is a way of teaching that facilitates children learning in natural settings. The whole language classroom provides an environment that encourages a child to develop physically, personally, socially, and cognitively. In a whole language classroom a wide variety of activities are provided respecting different cultural backgrounds, learning styles, and interests. Children are expected to take responsibility for their learning and to determine personal meaning from new information and ideas.

Whole language does not mean, "Today, students, we will be learning Standardized Test Skill #2214." It means finding a way to enroll the children in a whole story first and then attend to specific skills in a way that is meaningful to the child. It means putting aside all those ditto sheets for a while and getting involved in the story–more precisely, the message or theme of the story. Until you have the child's interest, specific skill learning will bore even the most motivated learner.

Whole language is an instructional philosophy that considers the way children learn language–oral language, written language, and body language. Body language? Yes, body language. Language is a system of communication that uses symbols, signs, and gestures. Language is a *body* of words and we communicate by thinking, listening, speaking, reading, writing, and *moving*. We've all heard of body language, haven't we? Emotions (affective domain) are expressed through the body. Watch children who are angry. How do they stand? How do they sit? They may stomp their feet or fold their arms or make angry faces. Watch children express joy and happiness. They dance, roll around on the ground, or jump for joy. Whole language instruction emphasizes that communication skills are learned by participating in a variety of meaningful experiences. Listening, speaking, reading, writing, and moving experiences are the activities that, when put together, comprise true whole language instruction.

The Whole Language Teacher

The whole language teacher knows that learning flourishes in an atmosphere where caring relationships are developed and trust flows both ways between the teacher and the student. The whole language teacher knows that nurturance encourages exploration and builds confidence. When a teacher is nurturing, it allows a child to be creative and to continuously grow and develop. The main goal of the whole language teacher is to be a "resource manager," responding to the student's needs and requirements. The whole language teacher arranges materials, resources, and experiences in order to better promote learning.

GA1501

The main functions of the whole language teacher are to:

- Develop learning experiences that have the potential to support the student.
- Plan for the use of materials that will allow the student to master learning tasks.
- Assist the student in the use of materials and resources provided.
- Monitor the student's use of provided materials and resources.
- Guide the student and offer information on progress made.

The Whole Language Student

The whole language teacher knows that the students are the genesis of all classroom teaching and activity. When considering the student in a whole language classroom, teaching is most effectively facilitated when we view the student as:

- Driven to seek knowledge and understanding.
- Capable and desirous of assuming increasingly more responsibility for learning.
- Satisfied with discovering something new, attaining new insights, and mastering new skills.
- Able to develop confidence and self-esteem as a result of the successful completion of learning tasks provided from real-life experiences that have personal meaning.

GA1501

Finding a Place for Self-Esteem Enhancement in the Curriculum

"Do what you can, with what you have, where you are."
- Theodore Roosevelt

If self-esteem is to be another add-on topic in an already overcrowded curriculum, its significance will be lost. However, if we develop a comprehensive plan by integrating particular processes into the curriculum, taking into consideration both the individual and the classroom environment, our job will be made much easier.

There are five steps or themes in the process of enhancing student self-esteem. Each step or theme builds upon the other in hierarchical style, enabling students to become self-empowered and intrinsically motivated. By incorporating all five themes throughout the school year, we will have acquired a comprehensive yearlong plan, or cycle, by which to integrate esteem-building activities into the curriculum. The five themes in this esteem-enhancing cycle are:

Building Trust	(pages 11-28)
Creating a Sense of Community	(pages 29-56)
Developing Self-Awareness	(pages 57-96)
Determining a Purpose	(pages 97-128)
Promoting Competence	(pages 129-155)

Ideally, each theme should be highlighted for approximately eight weeks; however, the actual length and duration of each theme will depend upon the students' development and direction in each area. Only when students have characterized each theme, or are acting consistently with the new value, will it be time to move on to the next step in this esteem-enhancing cycle. Remember to keep the focus on the students, not the lessons or activities. In a whole language classroom, the goal is to meet the needs of the students. Remember we teach children, not curriculum.

It is extremely important to remember that the teacher must allow as much time as necessary to establish a strong sense of trust for the students. This theme in the process is the foundation on which all the other themes rest. If a student is not able to trust the teacher, the other students, and the actual environment of the classroom, it is highly unlikely that the student will be able to move much further in his or her psychological and emotional development.

Allow time to build TRUST!

5

GA1501

Self-Esteem, Student Behavior, and Classroom Management

"Treat people as if they were what they ought to be,
and you help them become what they are capable of being."
- Goethe

When presenting cooperative or experiential activities to children, teachers must understand that children progress through different levels of social competency. A child with low self-esteem may be resistant and decide to act out when confronted with a "risky" type of social activity. If the child feels uncomfortable with the task, he or she doesn't think enough of him- or herself to believe that anything he or she contributes will be worthwhile.

Inevitably some of the children in your care will have an especially difficult time participating in some of the experiential and cooperative activities included in this book. This is due in part to the decisions they have made in regard to particular negative experiences in their lives. Because of perceived negative events, the children have acquired "life scripts" for themselves. These life scripts are usually something like, "There's something wrong with me," or "Nobody likes me." Let's take a look at how this can happen.

1. **Negative Experience: Inability to make someone happy.** At different times parents, teachers, or friends may not have been entirely consistent in the way they treated a child. At some time a child may have wanted to express and share him- or herself with significant others, but the parents, teacher, or friends did not accept or like what the child wanted to give. The child's efforts to please his or her significant others to gain their love and acceptance were not successful.

2. **Personal Decision: "I'm no good" or "I'll never win."** When this happens, children make decisions. Very often the decision is that they're no good, they can't win, or they can't please their parents, teachers, or friends.

3. **Solving the Problem: "How can I save myself?"** The child has decided that he or she is no good and can't possibly win, so the best thing to do is to find a way to keep from losing.

4. **Answer:** The child doesn't want to play or be involved, so he or she will look for a way to avoid participating fully, or a way to finally be accepted, such as:

- Refuse to play
- Quit the game
- Be a perfect player
- Kill the game
- Keep playing forever
- Make others lose
- Give excuses
- Try only
- Criticize others
- Don't finish the game
- I'll do everything for everybody

It's important to remember when dealing with children who show these tendencies to shape their behavior on a gradient. Start with an activity that is rather easy, something that leaves the child with an "out" so he or she doesn't feel pressured. If you don't, the child may panic and then react.

Life Scripts

GA1501

When the child becomes familiar with these activities, he or she will eventually progress to a competent social skill level. This is when the child feels comfortable performing most, if not all of the activities you present. Social skills will become automatic and transfer from one activity to another. The child becomes willing to take more risks and share more simply because of successful past experiences. Remember to be patient with children who are not capable of participating the "exact" way the activity requires. They're cooperating the best way they know how.

Here are the levels to consider when shaping a child's social behavior.

Level 1: Resistance–The child is resistant to any type of experiential activity you present. The child is just too scared to be involved.

Level 2: Awkwardness–The child is not sure how to behave and is apprehensive, "Should I, or shouldn't I?" Sometimes the child is willing to give it a try, but usually doesn't complete the activity.

Level 3: Hit or Miss–Sometimes a student is capable of performing the activity in the "right" way. Other times he or she returns to past resistant behavior.

Level 4: Transfer or Automatic–Social competency transfers to all experiential or cooperative activities. A student feels confident about his or her abilities to perform and is willing to risk.

Praising Appropriate Behavior

Students need to receive feedback that will let them know if their behavior is acceptable or inappropriate. Our communications (what we say and how we say it) can be very powerful tools toward creating positive change or very dangerous weapons that can cut away at a student's self-worth. Expressing our approval of students by awarding praise when deserved is a method towards enhancing self-esteem. Lets focus on the characteristics of giving praise effectively.

Praise must be:

1. **Deserved:** Kids know whether they deserve the praise they are receiving. Make sure the praise you are giving a student is deserved or else the child will be able to tell you are not sincere.

2. **Immediate:** If possible give the praising as soon as the action is performed. Your praise will have the greatest impact if given on the spot. Realize that public praisings are the best.

3. **Behavior-Centered:** In the beginning keep the praise focused on what action the student performed. Saying a student is pretty or nice may not coincide with current self-concept. Consequently, the praise will be met with resistance. It will be the student's desire to prove his or her negative self-concept right and your general evaluation wrong.

7

GA1501

4. **Specific:** Praise that lets a student know exactly what was done well is the most effective. When a student performs well, don't just say "good job" and leave it at that. Instead word your praising specifically by saying something like, "Jose, I'm impressed with the great job you did on your essay today because you capitalized every sentence and put a period at the end of every sentence also." If the student knows exactly what was done well, he or she is more likely to repeat the behavior in the future.

5. **Repeated:** For students whose self-esteem is very low, giving praise a couple of times may not be enough. Their self-concept may be very difficult to penetrate, so you may have to repeat the praise many times before the messages become internalized.

6. **Spontaneous:** Sometimes praising for the same behavior-centered action may be difficult to do without sounding like a message machine. When your praise sounds more spontaneous it will be much more effective.

7. **Describe Your Feeling:** Using statements such as, "I admire . . . ," or "I'm happy with . . . ," describe your thoughts or feelings in regard to your students' behavior. When you give praise in a way that describes how you are personally feeling, it is difficult for students to negate your statement. They would have a more difficult time saying, "No, you are not happy with the way I do my work quietly," or "You do not admire the way I wrote this story," rather than, "I did not do a good job." A student finds it very difficult to deflect your praise when given in a way that describes your feelings.

Brief Praisings

How about making an effort to catch students doing something right? Let's call this "Positive Pursuit." Look for good behavior, and when you find it, try these steps for a quick and effective praising:

1. Tell your students beforehand that you are going to let them know when they are doing well.
2. Actively pursue the positive; in other words, catch your students doing something right. And when you do, let them know right away how much you like and appreciate their behavior.
3. Tell your students exactly how you feel about what they did that inspired you to praise them. Describe your feeling.
4. Pause and allow a few seconds of silence to pass, to let them see how good you feel.
5. Tell them to keep up the good work.
6. Shake their hands or pat them gently on the back, letting them know that you support their efforts.

Responding to Inappropriate Behavior

It's important for teachers to understand why children act up when they do. We must understand that it's their behavior that's inappropriate–not their personhood. Although it may not seem like it at the time, kids usually have reasons for behaving the way they do. The two primary goals of children's inappropriate behavior are:

1. to fit in and belong.
2. to stand out as "special" or unique.

There are also secondary goals that inspire children's inappropriate behavior:

1. to get attention
2. to engage in a power struggle
3. to get back for hurts or punishments
4. to prove helplessness or inadequacy

Here are a few things to think about when noticing a child involved in inappropriate behavior.

Step 1: Ask yourself: "Is the child ignorant of the fact that the behavior is inappropriate?"
If yes, then educate–many times the child has no idea that he or she is misbehaving.
If no, then . . .

Step 2: Ask yourself: "Is the child unhappy?"
If yes, then discover the reason why and attend to the issue. Talk to the child; get to know him or her. Be a friend.
If no, then . . .

Step 3: Ask yourself: "Is the inappropriate behavior helping the child to achieve his or her goal?" Remember the two primary goals of inappropriate behavior are to fit in or to be special.

Getting Rid of Attention-Getting Behavior

This one is not always as simple as it sounds, but it stands to reason that if you do not respond to the child's inappropriate behavior it will eventually lead to extinction of that behavior. Take away the attention.

Eliminating the Power Struggle

When a child becomes engaged in a power struggle it is usually indicative of a deeper level of disturbance. Power struggles are still a result of the child's desire to either fit in or be special. The key to eliminating a power struggle is simply not to play the game. Convince yourself that there is wisdom in withdrawing from the power struggle. Remember, you can't have a fight if there is only one soldier on the battlefield.

GA1501

Removing Revenge-Seeking Behavior

When children have a habit of trying to get back for past hurts or punishments, it is sometimes indicative of an even deeper level of disturbance. Oftentimes abused children become involved in this revenge-seeking behavior. The best thing a teacher can do in this situation is to step aside from the punishment and not react. This takes away the payoff for the child. The worst thing that can happen is for the behavior to become cyclical: child is punished, child seeks revenge, child is punished, child seeks revenge, etc.

Cutting Off Helplessness

Helpless behavior is synonymous with attention-getting behavior. The child's reasoning is, "If the teacher does this for me then I'm special and I belong." The trouble is that if these kids continually receive reinforcement for this behavior, they may become chronic mental hospital patients. The key is to stay out of the child's feeling of helplessness. This is difficult for teachers to do; we want to save everybody! The best technique here is to break down the task into smaller, manageable pieces that the child can handle without your assistance. I know that at times this is difficult to accomplish, but with a little creativity and an abundance of patience, it can be done.

Brief Reprimands

How do you handle a student when he or she acts inappropriately? Here is a short, concise, and gentle way to reprimand a student without damaging his or her self-worth.

1. Reprimand the student as soon as possible.
2. Tell the student specifically what is unacceptable to you.
3. Explain to the student, in a very clear way, how you feel about the behavior.
4. Be silent for a few seconds. Let the student realize that you are indeed serious.
5. Simply tell your student that you will not accept the recent behavior, but you do like him or her.
6. Remind the student that he or she is a valuable and important person.
7. Let the student know the reprimand is over by touching him or her in a way that shows your support. A hand on the shoulder, a handshake, a pat on the back, or hug will do just fine.

"They may forget what you say,
but they never forget how you made them feel."
- John Hanley

Hey - I did that myself! I'm not helpless!

GA1501

Building Trust

"If you trust, you will be hurt, but if you don't trust, you will never learn to love."
– Mohandas Gandhi

Prerequisite of All Other Sources of Self-Esteem

Only when a child feels safe and secure will he or she be able to grow. A safe and secure classroom is a place where a child feels respected and accepted. It's a place where everyone is genuine and real, people tell it like it is, and the truth is always pursued. A child learns that he or she can trust when respectfully expressing concerns, feelings, doubts, and dreams without criticism or put-down. In a trusting classroom a child finds an abundance of nurturance and warmth, it feels good inside, and he or she wants to be there. In a trusting classroom a child knows what to expect; there are no inconsistencies or unwarranted surprises. A child learns that his or her opinion or vote is important and significant. Building trust is the first step and foundation for the enhancement of student self-esteem.

Building Trust with *The Velveteen Rabbit*

In order to build trust in our classrooms, we need to develop a trusting relationship with our students. To do this we must be willing to share a little more of ourselves. The process of enhancing self-esteem requires a sharing of thoughts, feelings, and experiences. For some, self-disclosure can be very difficult. It's much safer keeping to ourselves and not sharing our innermost thoughts and feelings. There is much less chance of getting hurt when we keep to ourselves, when we don't let others know of our insecurities or fears. However, if we're planning to ask our students to share of themselves, they need to trust us first. And in order to provide an environment of support, we must step outside our comfort zone, take a few risks, and share a part of ourselves. We must allow ourselves the opportunity to take off our "game face" and let the children see our real selves. When we share it's much easier for our students to do the same. The rewards are worth the risk.

Becoming Real isn't all that bad. Just ask someone wise and experienced like the Rabbit did to the old Skin Horse in Margery Williams' *The Velveteen Rabbit or How Toys Become Real.*

"What is REAL?" asked the Rabbit one day, when they were lying side by side near the nursery fender, before Nana came to tidy the room. "Does it mean having things that buzz inside you and a stick-out handle?"
"Real isn't how you are made," said the Skin Horse. "It's a thing that happens to you. When a child loves you for a long, long time, not just to play with, but *really* loves you, then you become Real."
"Does it hurt?" asked the Rabbit.
"Sometimes," said the Skin Horse, for he was always truthful. "When you are Real you don't mind being hurt.
"Does it happen all at once, like being wound up," he asked, "or bit by bit?"

GA1501

"It doesn't happen all at once," said the Skin Horse. "You become. It takes a long time. *That's why it doesn't often happen to people who break easily, or have sharp edges, or who have to be carefully kept.* Generally, by the time you are Real, most of your hair has been loved off, and your eyes drop out and you get loose in the joints and very shabby. But these things don't matter at all, because once you are Real you can't be ugly, except to people who don't understand."

Children understand. And we'll need to become resilient, soften up some, and get a little messy if we're going to touch our students' lives by becoming Real. Children want the truth, even if it hurts sometimes. They don't care to be lied to or hidden from the truth. *The Velveteen Rabbit* helps the teacher to explain that building trust requires a person to be truthful, to be honest, and to hold true to what has been said. Sometimes it's helpful to remember that you can fool a fool, you can con a con, but you can't kid a kid.

What follows is the literature-based thematic unit for developing the first step in the process of enhancing self-esteem, building trust.

Thematic Unit:	Trust
Core Literature:	*The Velveteen Rabbit* by Margery Williams (Henry Holt & Co.)
Extended Literature:	*Hug Me* by Patty Stren (Harper & Row)
	Koko's Kitten by Francine Patterson (Scholastic)
Recreational Literature:	*The Complete Adventures of Peter Rabbit* by Beatrix Potter (Frederick Wayne & Co., Inc.)
	Peter Rabbit's Natural Foods Cookbook by Arnold Dobrin, illustrated by Beatrix Potter (Frederick Wayne & Co., Inc.)
	The Tale of Peter Rabbit by Beatrix Potter (Frederick Wayne & Co., Inc.)

Additional Literature Supporting the Theme of Trust

Alexander and the Terrible, Horrible, No Good, Very Bad Day by Judith Viorst (Atheneum)
Annie and the Old One by Miska Miles (Little, Brown)
Blue Willow by Doris Gates (Viking Press)
But Names Will Never Hurt Me by Bernard Waber (Houghton Mifflin)
Corduroy by Don Freeman (Viking Children's Books)
Emperor's New Clothes by Hans Christian Andersen (Four Winds)
It's Mine by Leo Lionni (Alfred A. Knopf)
The Little Brute Family by Russell Hoban (Dell Publishing Co., Inc.)
The Napping House by Audrey Wood (Harcourt Brace Jovanovich)
The Pushcart War by Jean Merrill (Dell Publishing Co., Inc.)
Runaway Bunny by Margaret W. Brown (HarperCollins)
Strega Nona by Tomie de Paola (Simon & Schuster)
Sylvester and the Magic Pebble by William Steig (Simon & Schuster)
Where the Wild Things Are by Maurice Sendak (HarperCollins)

GA1501

Supporting Subthemes of Trust

The following subthemes help to support or complement building trust, the first step of enhancing self-esteem. Subthemes provide a tangent for either the teacher or the students to take when developing understanding of the theme of trust.

- Basic Needs
- Accepting Change
- Law
- Liberty
- Life
- Death
- Safety
- Limits

- Power
- Punishment
- Truth
- Self-Disclosure
- Faith
- Acceptance
- Security
- Honesty

- Genuineness
- Dependability
- Integrity
- Openness
- Sincerity
- Honor
- Shelter

Self-Esteem Theme Objectives

The teacher will . . .

1. **Develop a trusting relationship with students.** The first value that the responsible teacher wants to develop with his or her students is a trusting relationship. You want children to feel comfortable with you so they will come to you with their questions and concerns, to know that they can count on you. The two most important ingredients in building trust are honesty and openness. Through the act of self-disclosure the teacher in the classroom functions as a facilitator towards creating conditions favorable for self-expansion. If you are to build trust, you must model "realness" by letting your students know how you feel, letting them know what sort of mistakes you have made, letting them know a little something about yourself. Building trust also means "busting" your students on their "stuff." This means honestly letting them know what you think of their behavior, telling them when you know they are trying to manipulate you. If students know they can get you to "jump through a hoop" for them, they will have a hard time trusting you. Children want you to be honest with them.
2. **Create an environment based on safety and security.** Create a predictable routine within the classroom that children can depend upon. We want a calm classroom with predictable events. Later on when the children feel safe and secure, then we can get a little "crazy" with our day or lessons.
3. **Set reasonable "agreements."** Create a lesson whereby everyone in the room becomes involved in the rule-making process. This way children have had a voice in what happens in the room. Perhaps we can call them "agreements," not rules. Children feel much more comfortable with agreements. Once you have established classroom agreements, make sure you do your best to keep them consistently enforced. Nothing creates more distrust than inconsistent consequences or rewards. If a child receives consequences for inappropriate behavior in one instance, and in another occurrence of the same inappropriate behavior, it is allowed, children will become confused and distrustful.
4. **Create a positive and caring environment.** "What does it mean to care?" "What is it like to have a positive environment?" These are just two of the lessons that you can create, or questions to ask the students, in order to teach trust in your classroom.
5. **Promote a democratic environment.** As much as possible, involve the children in the decision-making process. Provide alternatives that the children can vote on; let the majority rule. Kids will feel as though their attitudes and opinions count.

The students will . . .
- Feel comfortable and safe while in the care of your classroom.
- Understand what is expected of them and you.
- Be able to depend on individuals and situations.
- Understand that there are rules and limits within your classroom.

Interpersonal Activities That Build Trust

Boasting Buddies

Goal: Students will describe positive personality traits and build empathy for others in challenging situations.

Time: 10-15 minutes

Setting: Classroom

Materials: None

Procedure: Have each student find a partner. Try to persuade students to pick someone that they don't know very well. Have the partners sit facing each other with their knees almost touching. Then have the partners decide who will be partner A and who will be partner B. Tell the students, "Now you will have ninety seconds to tell your partner what you like, love, appreciate, respect, and admire most about– yourself." Before beginning, ask your students: "Who is feeling a little bit nervous right now?" "Why?" Then it is generally a good idea for you to demonstrate or model the exercise in front of the group. By doing the activity first you will be helping to make it okay for your students to do the same. Plus, they will want to hear your statements as well. Finally, surprise them by having partner B start first. Smile when you listen to all the moaning. Make sure you remind your students that they should be telling their listening partners their attributes, accomplishments, and achievements. Afterward ask your students, "Now that we are finished, how many of you feel a little closer or friendlier to your partner?" Tell them the reason why is that now they know a little more about their partners and they all survived this "scary" activity.

I appreciate the kindness I show to people.

My Life Story

Goal: Students will become more aware of positive life experiences and improve their ability to disclose personal information in a trusting environment.

Time: 10-15 minutes

Setting: Classroom

Materials: None

Procedure: Ask your students to get together with a partner they haven't worked with yet. Have the partners sit facing each other with their knees almost touching. Decide who is to be partner A and who will be partner B. Explain that they will each have ninety seconds to tell "their life story." Explain that there are two ways to tell your story. One way is negative, telling about all the bad things that have happened throughout your lifetime. The other way is positive, telling about all the good things that have happened in your lifetime. Then model or demonstrate the two types of autobiographical storytelling, ending with the positive story. This activity usually brings up all types of discussion, and many students realize that they have much in common. Remember that the storytelling should be positive so that all participants become more aware of all the good in their lives.

GA1501

Sharing Secrets

Goal: Students will be able to disclose one item of personal information with the whole group.

Time: 10-15 minutes

Setting: Classroom

Materials: Index cards for each student, pencils, large paper bag

Procedure: Have your students write secrets about themselves on index cards. Make sure you tell them not to write their names on the cards. Tell them to write something they wouldn't mind telling others, such as, "I'm afraid of heights." After all the students have completed their cards, drop the "secrets" into a large paper bag. When all the cards are in the bag, have your students take turns picking out a card and reading the secret aloud. The class can try to guess to whom the secret belongs. When all the cards have been read, and all the secrets have been disclosed, the students can discuss how they felt when sharing the secrets.

Encounter

Goal: Students will describe classmates in a positive way.

Time: 30-40 minutes

Setting: Room enough to move around freely

Materials: Construction paper, clothespins, pencils, crayons

Procedure: Pass out a large piece of construction paper to all your students. Then tell them to write five or ten words that describe their good characteristics on one side of the paper (tell them that they can decorate the words if they wish). Then pass out the clothespins and have each student attach the piece of paper to the back of his or her shirt at the collar. The paper should be pinned on the back so that the blank side is exposed. Then have your students roam around the room with a crayon, making sure they get to everyone to write a one-word description or adjective of the person whose back they are writing on. Explain that the word written should be one that describes how that person is to you. Depending on the maturity of the group, you might want to explain that comments written are to be only positive ones. After each person has had time to write a word on the back of everyone participating, students return to their seats and compare how they see themselves with how others see them. Follow it up with a discussion.

Blind Sitting

Goal: Express feelings, break the ice, increase self-awareness.

Time: 10-15 minutes

Setting: Room large enough to move around comfortably, chairs or desks

Materials: None

Procedure: The students in the classroom all stand in a tight bunch in the center of the room. When everyone is standing quietly and still, have everyone close his or her eyes and tell students to find a place in the room to sit down. Explain that they must not open their eyes, so they must walk slowly and carefully as they go anywhere in the room they wish. After everyone is seated the students may open their eyes and look around the room. Discussion begins as to why they chose their places to sit down. "Why did you sit so close to or far away from everyone?"

Variation: Have several members trade positions and describe their feelings sitting in someone else's place.

GA1501

The Trust Target

Goal: Self-awareness, identifying the people that we disclose different levels of information to in order to obtain support.

Time: 20-30 minutes

Setting: Classroom

Materials: Construction paper, pencils, crayons, markers

Procedure: Students construct a "Target of Trust" drawing. The drawing is made with six concentric circles (one around another like a target). In the center circle the children write the word *Myself,* in the second circle the children write *Family,* in the third circle the children write *Friends,* in the fourth circle *Classroom Mates,* in the fifth circle *Teacher,* and in the sixth and largest circle write *Strangers.* The smallest and center circle is the closest one to each of them, *Myself.* The teacher writes the following statements on the board and asks the students to think of whom they would share the situation with. Then after the students draw their Trust Targets, tell them to write the situation number or the situation statement inside the circle of which they would be comfortable sharing the experience or situation with.

Situations: (1) Giggle with . . . (2) Tell secrets to . . . (3) Get angry at . . . (4) Be sad and cry in front of . . . (5) Ask for help from . . . (6) Share lunch with . . . (7) Ask to borrow money from . . . (8) Ask for a ride home from . . . (9) Bring home . . . (10) Tell problems to . . .

Discussion follows that suggests ways to increase support available to the students.

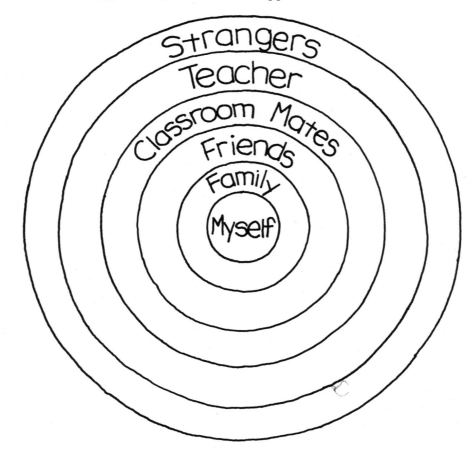

GA1501

Trust Walk

Goal: Students will learn to trust fellow classmates and develop empathic understanding.
Time: 20 to 30 minutes
Setting: The classroom or, if you're feeling bold enough, the hallway
Materials: Enough blindfolds for half of the class
Procedure: Explain to the class that trust means belief or knowing of the honesty and integrity of another person or thing. It means feeling confident in someone or something else. It can also mean feeling confident in yourself, that you can trust yourself. Next ask the class, "What kinds of things does a person do to be considered trustworthy?" Cluster their responses around the word *trustworthy* on the board. Responses will be telling the truth, keeping secrets, caring, understanding, keeping commitments, etc. Next ask the students, "Whom can you trust?" Some of them might say their parents, older brother or sister (if they're lucky), or special friends. Then ask them, "How many of you would like to develop more trusting relationships with other children in this class?" Almost everyone raises his or her hand. Your response should be, "Good, because we're going to do this special trust-building exercise today."

Explain to the class that they are going to participate in a Trust Walk. Then explain that this is a very special activity and it must be completed with the utmost of care and concern for everyone involved. If anyone doesn't think he or she can handle this activity, that student should be given the opportunity to sit this one out. Say that if he or she is not feeling trustful that it is okay to sit back and watch during this time. Then ask the class, "Is there anyone here who would like to develop a more trusting relationship with another person in the room? Would anyone like to develop a new friendship or improve on an existing friendship?" Lots of children will raise their hands. Call on them and ask whom they would like to work with on building trust. Pair the children up by having the "picker" stand behind the chair of the "pickee." Do this until all the children have been paired up.

Now with the "pickers" standing behind the "pickees," explain to the children that all the pickers will receive blindfolds to tie around the pickees' eyes so they can't see. Explain, "Once the blindfolds are on, the pickers will help the pickees to stand up, and the pickers will then proceed to lead the pickees around the room. The pickees will be walking blindfolded." Invariably the kids are excited! Tell them, "This is a very special activity and special care must be taken in order to help the blindfolded person feel safe, so that he or she will be able to trust you." Ask, "Is it a good idea for you to lead your partner around the room and bump into something?" No. "Is it a good idea, if you want your partner to trust you, to poke and laugh at him or her?" No. "Is it a good idea to lead your partner around the room at a pace that is faster than he or she feels comfortable with?" No. "Good, then I think we're ready to begin." They're all excited now, so it's a good idea to just stand and wait patiently for them to be calm and realize that you mean business when you say that we have to do this very carefully.

Pass out the blindfolds to the pickers and have the pickers tie them onto the pickees. Then check the blindfolds to make sure they are on tightly so the others can't see. Now the pickers should be standing behind the pickees. The pickees have the blindfolds on, and the pickers should have their hands gently on the shoulders of the pickees. Then have the pickers slowly stand the pickees up and lead them slowly around the room. Explain that they can allow the blindfolded people to touch things and to explore. Then have the children eventually set the blindfolders down anywhere in the room. When everyone is sitting down quietly, ask the blindfolded people if they can guess where they are sitting. It's kind of fun to see if they can tell. Everyone likes it. Ask the blindfolded people if they feel comfortable and safe. Some of them will say yes, others no. Then have the pickers take the blindfolds off of the pickees.

Ask questions now like, "Did you feel comfortable with your partner?" "Do you feel like you can trust him or her?" "Was it fun walking around blindfolded?" "Do you feel closer with your partner now?"

Then do the same for the other group of students. Sometimes it's good to wait until the next day for the other half of the students to be blindfolded. Perhaps now you could pair up the students as "buddies" for the rest of the day, each of them helping another and developing a friendship. For an extension, have the children write about the experience or draw the experience.

GA1501

Journal Writing for Building Trust

Journal writing is talking with one's self in a way that offers a concrete expression of thoughts, feelings, and ideas. Writing in a personal journal can be a valuable tool for self-understanding and more skillful writing. When journal entries are incorporated in classroom instruction on a regular basis, it will also become an ongoing account of personal growth. Journal writing can be a quiet time of day for self-reflection and for bringing closure to prior activities. Try it at the beginning of the day, after recess, or before lunch. Construct your own journals or use one of the many types provided by different school suppliers.

Student self-esteem journals need to be confidential, and the thoughts and feelings that students write should never be read by you or other students unless permission is granted. At the end of each journal-writing activity you may wish to ask if anyone would like to read what was written. Some children will want to share their journal entries each time, and others will remain private. It is also a good idea to explain to students that their journals will not be corrected for spelling or grammar. Their thoughts and ideas are what count most. Tell them that if they don't know how to spell a word to just invent their own spelling.

To get started, just write one of these trust-building sentence stems on the board and invite the children to do the rest.

- A person that I can trust is . . .
- My vote counts because . . .
- I trust people best when I . . .
- When someone talks nicely to me I feel . . .
- Some of the people that I care about are . . .
- When I'm around a lot of people, I like to . . .
- I can trust other people because . . .
- The reason why we set "agreements" is . . .
- I can tell my parents about . . .
- What I like about our classroom is . . .
- I wish I could change . . .
- When I let others know how I feel they . . .
- I earn others' trust by . . .

- I feel safe when . . .
- I trust people best when they . . .
- I am being honest when . . .
- I can tell a secret to . . .
- When I say good things about myself I feel . . .
- My teacher helps me feel safe by . . .
- I can tell my friends about . . .
- If I were in charge of this school I would . . .
- Sometimes I don't trust people because . . .
- I can tell my teacher about . . .
- I feel special when . . .
- When I'm alone I like to . . .
- Other people are important because . . .

GA1501

Interdisciplinary Activities

Language Arts

The "Stuffie" Adventure!

Goal: To use speaking and writing communication skills for the purpose of building empathy in group experiences.

Time: Several days, dependent on the number of students involved

Setting: Your classroom

Materials: Various publishing materials, such as writing papers, pencils, crayons, markers, binding materials, laminating machine, etc.

Procedure: First, if you have a stuffed animal at home, take it to school. After reading with the class a portion of *The Velveteen Rabbit*, take the time to display your "stuffie." Being a good model for your students, share the personal story of you and your "stuffie." When finished, invite the students, as a homework assignment, to bring their own stuffed animals to school so that they can share them with the rest of the class. Second, the next day after reading more in *The Velveteen Rabbit*, ask the students to talk about their "stuffies." Ask, "What's your stuffie's name?" "What kinds of things do you do with it?" "Do you sleep with it?" "Did someone give you your stuffed animal?" "How is it like the stuffed animals in the story?" Third, encourage the children to write adventure stories involving themselves and their stuffed animals as the main characters. Put the finished published stories (with book covers, title page, illustrations, bindings, etc.) in the classroom library and provide a time for students to read one another's stories or to share their stories with the class. Make sure to continue your talk about trust as it appears in the stories the students have written and how trustful they felt or didn't feel as they shared their personal stories about their "stuffies."

Health

The Juice Party

Goal: Students will understand that a balanced program of nutritional diet, exercise, recreation, and rest contributes to cardiovascular fitness, health, and self-esteem.

Time: Approximately one hour

Setting: Your classroom

Materials: Teacups, paper plates, napkins, and nutritious snacks, such as juice, fruit, whole wheat crackers, cheese

Procedure: Have your students gather their stuffed animals. Explain that in order to be healthy we need to take care of ourselves. Proper health means eating good foods, exercising, playing, and getting adequate rest. Then explain that with our stuffies we are going to have a healthy "juice" party. Proceed to pass out the cups, plates, napkins, assorted fruits, and juices. Enjoy eating the healthy foods. When done, clean up while teaching how being clean contributes to good health. Then explain that now is the time for exercise and fun. Ask, "How do bunny rabbits travel or go from place to place?" The kids will answer, "They hop!" "Great, now clear a pathway so everyone can do a Follow the Leader Bunny Hop." While you're at it try some other physical activities like a "Bunny Rabbit Jumping Jack" or whatever else you can think of. Finally, explain that good health activities always end with a little rest period, so have the children get their stuffed animals and return to their area so that they can take a short nap. Gently wake them up to discuss and review the good health process.

GA1501

Science

Rabbit Salad Lunch

Goal: Students will learn that each kind of living thing gets what it needs from the environment and is interdependent with many other living things.

Time: Several days

Setting: Your classroom and the school library

Materials: Encyclopedias, books on rabbits and their habitats, tagboard, writing materials, salad bowl, plates, utensils, salad foods

Procedure: First, you'll want to research and discover several different types of rabbits; Old English, Angora, and Dutch are just a few. Perhaps the students can draw pictures of the rabbits and write a short report. In the report make sure they include information about the life cycle of rabbits and their natural environment. Next, get *Peter Rabbit's Natural Foods Cookbook* by Arnold Dobrin, illustrated by Beatrix Potter, in order to make a "Rabbit Salad" with your students. Facilitate a discussion about the different types of vegetables included in the salad. Ask your students, "What type of food does a rabbit eat?" Ultimately, it would be a great idea if you had a real live rabbit in your classroom to share your "Rabbit Salad" with. Many school districts have rabbits available for checkout or borrowing at their science centers, and if you don't have a science center, the local pet shop is sure to have a rabbit that the whole class could purchase if necessary. Having a pet rabbit in your classroom is a great way to facilitate learning about a rabbit's environment and about the interdependence of all living things. How good do you feel taking care of a cute little bunny rabbit?

Math

Measuring Up

Goal: Students will understand that measurement allows us to assign a number to a specific quantity according to the properties of what is measured. Students will express temperature of the body, boiling water, and freezing water.

Time: Several days

Materials: Various types of thermometers, hot plate, cooking pot, paper and pencils

Procedure: In our story the little boy becomes ill with scarlet fever. Scarlet fever is an infectious disease that chiefly affects children and sometimes precedes rheumatic fever. The little boy had a fever so hot that it burned the rabbit! What a great opportunity to have a health lesson lead into a math lesson on measurement. Now all you need are some thermometers (check with your school nurse) to take the temperature of several students in your room. Have the children estimate what their temperatures will be. Then write the results on the board. Next do the same with boiling water and then ice water. Graph your results. Then finally have the children take turns measuring the temperature of various things in your room. Graph those findings as well. Make sure they have been taught how to read a thermometer properly of course, and have them learn these temperature norms:

Body Temperature	Boiling Temperature	Freezing Temperature
98.6 Fahrenheit	212 Fahrenheit	32 Fahrenheit
37.0 Celsius	100 Celsius	0 Celsius

Is Your Toy Real?

Think of all the wonderful toys that you have had. Is there any one toy that is very, very special to you? Would you like your toy to be Real? Draw a picture of yourself playing with your toy. In this picture pretend that your toy is Real.

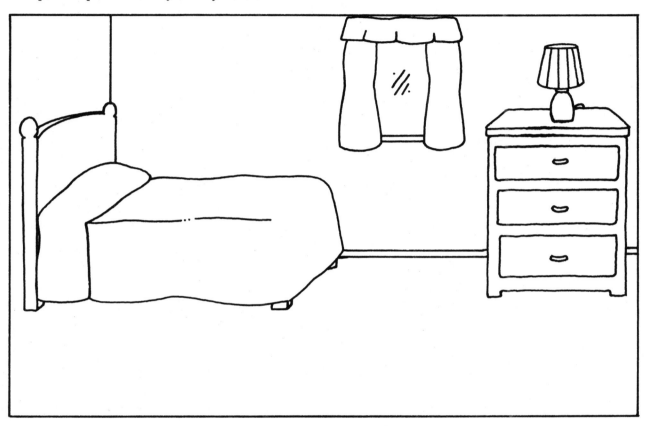

Now write a short story about the picture above. Where were you when you were with your Real toy? What were you doing that was so special?

_____

_____

_____

_____

_____

_____

GA1501

The Old Skin Horse

The old Skin Horse lived in the nursery longer than any of the other toys. What kinds of words are used to describe the old Skin Horse in the story?

_____

How does the Skin Horse say that toys become Real?

_____

Does it hurt to become Real?

_____

How long does the Skin Horse tell us it takes to become Real?

_____

How did the Skin Horse become Real?

_____

Once a toy becomes Real how long does it stay Real?

_____

Would you be a friend to the old Skin Horse? Why?

_____

_____

GA1501

Does the Velveteen Rabbit Feel?

How do you think the Velveteen Rabbit felt in the beginning of the story when he was really special? He was new when he was put in the boy's stocking on Christmas morning.

_____

_____

_____

How do you think the Velveteen Rabbit felt when he was living in the nursery with the old Skin Horse? He was very quiet and no one thought very much about him then.

_____

_____

_____

How do you think the Velveteen Rabbit felt when he was picked up by Nana and given to the little boy to sleep with?

_____

_____

_____

How do you think the Velveteen Rabbit felt when he had to wait in the garbage pile behind the chicken house to be set on fire?

_____

_____

How do you think the Velveteen Rabbit felt when he was kissed by the Fairy and finally became Real?

_____

_____

GA1501

Rabbitland

The little Velveteen Rabbit is brought into the woods by the lovely Fairy. The Fairy kisses him and he becomes Real. Now he is to be a new playmate for all the rabbits in Rabbitland where he will live forever and ever. The other rabbits must be very kind to him and teach him all they know. What kinds of things will they teach him? What kind of "agreements" will the rabbits live by? What will he do now that he lives in Rabbitland?

_____

_____

_____

_____

_____

_____

_____

_____

_____

Draw a picture of the Real rabbit in Rabbitland.

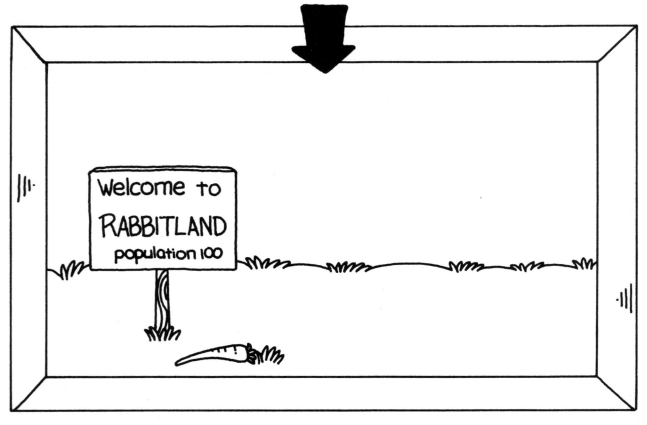

GA1501

Imagine!

Imagine that you are now the Real Rabbit. Imagine that you are watching the little boy playing in the woods. You are now Real and you haven't seen the boy for a long time. What is the little boy doing? How does he look now? How do you feel now that you are Real? Draw a picture of you as the Real Rabbit watching the little boy playing in the woods. When you finish drawing the picture write a short story telling what you see and how you feel.

_____

_____

_____

_____

_____

_____

GA1501

People I Can Trust

How many people do you know that you can trust?

How do you know when you can trust people?

Write the names of people that you can trust and tell why. Then draw a picture of those trustful people doing something important with you.

I can trust _____

because _____

_____

I can trust _____

because _____

_____

I can trust_____

because _____

_____

I can trust _____

because _____

_____

I can trust_____

because _____

_____

I can trust _____

because _____

_____

GA1501

"Agreements"

What do you want your classroom to be like? How do you want everyone to be treated? Do you want a noisy classroom or a quiet classroom? Do you want a messy classroom or a clean classroom? Do you want to learn? Do you want to feel important?

Hmmm.... How do I want my classroom?

You are important! Important enough for your opinions and thoughts to count. Now is the time to decide how you want your classroom to be. You get to decide what is important for your classroom!

Write six words that describe the way you want your classroom to be. Here are a few examples: calm, orderly, peaceful.

_____   _____   _____

_____   _____   _____

Now write six "Agreements" or ways of behaving that you are willing to live by in your classroom. When you set "Agreements" they take the place of rules. Is it a good idea for people to raise their hands to be called on to speak? Is it a good idea for people to put their trash in the wastebasket?

What do you think?

1. _____

2. _____

3. _____

4. _____

5. _____

6. _____

Now, work with your teacher to decide together what type of
"Agreements" everyone will live by in your classroom.
Share with the class what you wrote.
Your opinion is important!

GA1501

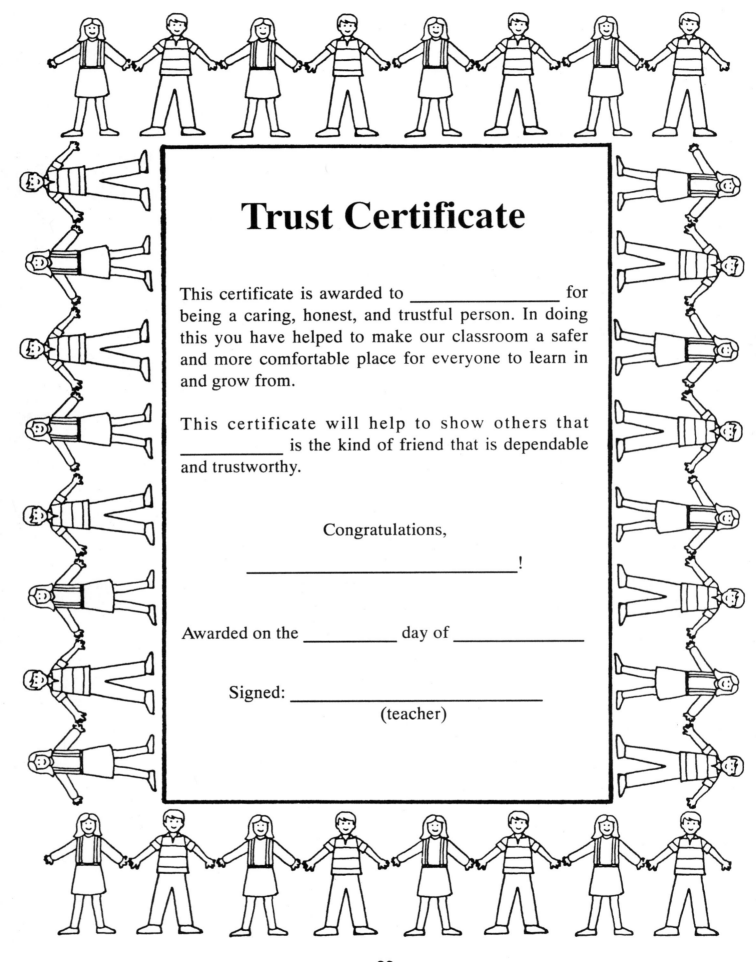

Trust Certificate

This certificate is awarded to _____ for being a caring, honest, and trustful person. In doing this you have helped to make our classroom a safer and more comfortable place for everyone to learn in and grow from.

This certificate will help to show others that _____ is the kind of friend that is dependable and trustworthy.

Congratulations,

_____!

Awarded on the _____ day of _____

Signed: _____
(teacher)

Creating a Sense of Community

"I get by with a little help from my friends. I'm gonna try with a little help from my friends."
– The Beatles

Build a Classroom Coalition

With the trustful classroom that you have created you notice now that the children seem to feel comfortable. They understand the agreements which have been consistently enforced, they can come to you with their concerns, and they find that they can rely on their fellow classmates as well. Now you want to begin to work on the next step in the process. You want to create an alliance, or coalition, whereby all the members of the classroom will merge their efforts towards the acquisition of common goals, forming a union. When the class works together on each individual's growth and progress through group goals, students develop friendships. Friends and peers have an enormous influence on our feelings of worth. When a child hears from another, "I like you; you're my friend. Come along with us," he or she feels valued and important. A child feels good when included and feels like he or she belongs. When this feeling is a part of the classroom, a community has been created.

Creating a Sense of Community with *Charlotte's Web*

The most beloved modern animal fantasy of our time, *Charlotte's Web* by E.B. White, does an excellent job supporting the theme of belonging. This is a lovely story about how a loyal spider named Charlotte A. Cavatica befriends and saves the life of a humble pig named Wilbur. Through the challenging interactions on the Zuckerman farm, *Charlotte's Web* reveals the true meaning of loneliness and the obligations of friendship.

One day a kindly old sheep casually informs Wilbur that as soon as he is nice and fat he will be butchered. When Wilbur becomes hysterical, Charlotte promises to save him. She does so by miraculously spinning words into her web that describe Wilbur as "radiant," "terrific" and "humble," making him famous. Wilbur, who has been accepted and is now loved by all the farm animals, is eventually saved, but poor old Charlotte dies alone in the fairgrounds. Fortunately Wilbur, who has learned the meaning of community, manages to bring Charlotte's egg sac back to the farm so that the continuation of life in the barnyard is maintained. Even though Wilbur loves her children and grandchildren dearly, he never forgets his wise friend Charlotte. Because of Charlotte's friendship and the way she accepted him warmly, he can look forward to living a long and pleasant life.

"Life in the barn was very good—night and day, winter and summer, spring and fall, dull days and bright days. It was the best place to be, thought Wilbur, this delicious cellar, with the garrulous geese, the changing seasons, the heat of the sun, the passage of swallows, the nearness of rats, the sameness of sheep, the love of spiders, the smell of manure, and the glory of everything." [1]

---

1. From CHARLOTTE'S WEB by E.B. White. Copyright © 1952. Text copyright renewed 1980. Reprinted by permission of HarperCollins Publishers, New York, New York.

Wilbur is surely in a place where he feels he belongs. This story, with its humor, wisdom and beauty, keeps us in touch with the warm feelings of community and friendship.

Thematic Unit:	Community
Core Literature:	*Charlotte's Web* by E.B. White (HarperCollins)
Extended Literature:	*The Hating Book* by Charlotte Zolotow (HarperTrophy)
	The Hundred Dresses by Eleanor Estes (Harcourt Brace Jovanovich)
	The Stone Faced Boy by Paula Fox (Aladdin)

Additional Literature Supporting the Theme of Community

Amos and Boris by William Steig (Puffin)
Arthur's Pen Pal by Lillian Hoban (Harper & Row)
Bedtime for Francis by Russell Hoban (Harper & Row)
Best Friends by Steven Kellogg (Dial Books for Young Readers)
Blueberries for Sal by Robert McClosky (Viking)
A Book of Hugs by Dave Ross (Thomas Y. Crowell)
Chester's Way by Kevin Henkes (Greenwillow Books)
Cricket in Times Square by George Selden (Cornerstone Books)
Dexter by Clyde Robert Bulla (Crowell)
Friends by Helme Heine (Atheneum)
Frog and Toad Are Friends by Arnold Lobel (Harper & Row)
The Giving Tree by Shel Silverstein (HarperCollins)
A House for Hermit Crab by Eric Carle (Picture Book Studio)
Ira Sleeps Over by Bernard Waber (Houghton Mifflin)
James and the Giant Peach by Roald Dahl (Bantam Book)
King of the Wind by Marguerite Henry (Checkerboard Press)
Let's Be Enemies by Janice May Udry; illustrated by Maurice Sendak (Harper)
A Letter to Amy by Ezra Jack Keats (Harper & Row)
Little House in the Big Woods by Laura Ingalls Wilder (HarperCollins)
The Little Red Hen by Paul Galdone (Clarion Books/Ticknor & Fields)
May I Bring a Friend by Beatrice Schenk de Reginiers (Atheneum)
Rabbit Hill by Robert Lawson (Viking)
Ramona and Her Father by Beverly Cleary (Morrow)
Rock Finds a Friend by Randall J. Wiethorn (Green Tiger Press, Inc.)
Sam by Ann Herbert Scott (McGraw Hill)
Sarah, Plain and Tall by Patricia MacLachlan (Harper & Row)
Stevie by John Steptoe (HarperCollins)
Stone Soup by Marcia Brown (Scribner)
Teammates by Peter Golenbock (Harcourt Brace Jovanovich)
Winnie the Pooh by Alan Alexander Milne (E.P. Dutton)
Year at Maple Hill Farm by Alice Provensen (Atheneum)
Yonder by Tony Johnston (Dial Books for Young Readers)

GA1501

Supporting Subthemes of Community

The following subthemes help to support or complement creating a sense of community, the second step of enhancing self-esteem. Subthemes provide a tangent for either the teacher or the students to take when developing understanding of the theme of community.

- Communication
- Conflict
- Culture
- Democracy
- Family
- Citizen
- World
- Cooperation
- Togetherness

- Love
- Interaction
- Interdependence
- Relations
- Friends
- Ecosystems
- Universe
- Compassion
- Union

- Coalition
- Team
- Neighborhood
- Gang
- Inclusion
- Belonging
- Group
- Habitats

Self-Esteem Theme Objectives

The teacher will . . .
1. **Promote inclusion within the group.** Is everyone included in everything you do? Do you allow certain children to sit out on the bench during particular activities in P.E.? Is everyone reading the same story, or do you have reading groups where some of the children are reading out of a lower level book? Does everyone feel like this is a place to belong?
2. **Provide opportunities to discover one another.** "Wow, I'm beginning to learn all about my classmates. I'm finding out that they're just like me in a lot of ways!" "I know their cultural backgrounds and what their interests are. In a lot of ways, we have many things in common!" Children need to recognize their similarities and to feel responded to by others.
3. **Incorporate cooperative games and activities.** Slowly introduce the children to cooperative activities. Take every precaution to set them up so that the children will be successful in their cooperative efforts. The task should be easy enough so that everyone will succeed with very little or no conflict developing between students. Try the Silent Team Puzzle to set the tone for quiet, safe, cooperative efforts.
4. **Develop group identity.** Form cooperative groups where all the children sit together in the group throughout the day. Have a fun game where the children make up a name for their group. Have the children pick buddies that will take care of getting their homework if one of them misses a day. Encourage peer approval, acceptance, and support by providing activities that help to increase children's skills in friendship making.
5. **Model the 5 A's: attention, acceptance, approval, acknowledgement, and affection.** Each child needs to receive an abundance of these five A's from the teacher. The teacher must realize that behavior of a child may not always be appropriate, and we don't have to approve or accept it, but the child must understand that it is the behavior that is not acceptable or approved of, not him or her.

The students will . . .
- Learn that they are in a place where they are wanted and belong.
- Feel respected and valued by others.
- Develop a sense of classroom and school spirit and pride.

GA1501

Cooperation Activities

Silent Team Puzzle

Goal: Each member will participate with a group to form five 6" (15.24 cm) squares from puzzle pieces.

Time: 30 minutes

Setting: The classroom

Materials: Five puzzles per group, measuring 6" x 6" (15.24 x 15.24 cm), containing three pieces each, within a large manilla envelope

Procedure: This game is a great way to help students become more aware of group behaviors which promote effective teamwork. Begin by asking your students, "What are some of the ways we all communicate without talking?" Write their answers on the board. Some of their responses may include pointing a finger, waving a hand, nodding one's head, etc. Then ask, "What do we call this kind of communicating?" Answer, "Body language." Finally ask, "What is necessary for cooperation when people work together to complete a task? In other words, what does it mean to cooperate?" Again write their responses on the board.

Next distribute the pieces to the five puzzles in the large manilla envelopes. Explain to the teams that they must put together the pieces so that they end up with five equal-sized squares each containing three pieces. Explain that there is to be no talking during the time each group is putting together the puzzles. The object of the game is to be the first team to put together all five puzzles without talking. Having your students work together cooperatively in a silent manner at first will help to set the tone for further "quiet" learning situations.

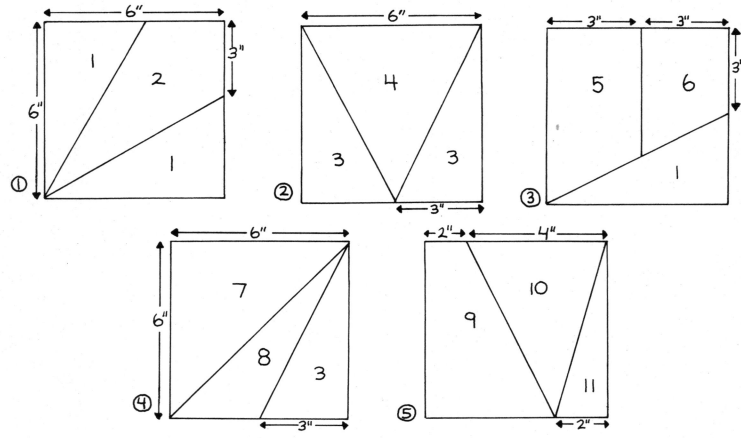

GA1501

Billowing Blankets

Goal: Students will work together in order to promote a sense of fellowship.

Time: 30 minutes

Setting: Playground or volleyball court

Materials: Two playground balls and two blankets

Procedure: First, spread out two sturdy blankets on the ground (the blankets are going to get dirty, so don't plan on using them for anything important in the future). Divide the class into two teams and have the two teams spread out around the two blankets. Each team then grabs the edges of the blanket and lifts the blanket off the ground, holding it at waist level, stretching it out to its full size. A large playground ball is then placed in the middle of each blanket. Teams then practice tossing the ball into the air and catching it again in the center of the blanket. Each team must work together to attempt to throw and catch the ball at the same time, otherwise the ball will not lift very far off the blanket. Once each team is able to work together to toss the ball successfully up into the air and catch it, teams can then pass one ball back and forth. One team tosses the ball up into the air and the other team manuevers so they catch the ball in their blanket. Later, when the teams are successfully tossing the ball back and forth, a game can begin in which each team is defending one side of a volleyball court. Each team attempts to throw the ball over the net to the other side. Points can be scored for each successful catch made or each time the ball drops on the other side without being caught. This game is very cooperative in nature, as every team member must work to be a part of every toss and every catch made by the team.

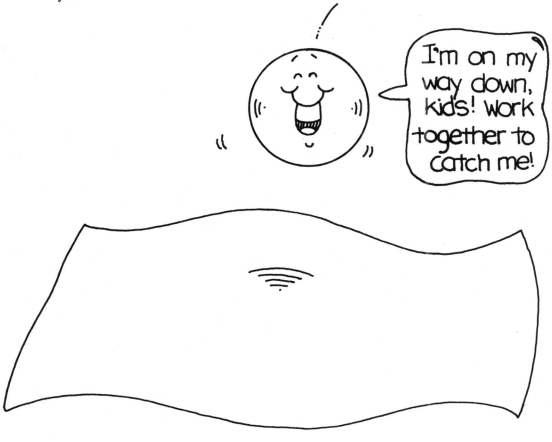

GA1501

Silent Drawing

Goal: Students will learn to cooperate with classmates to complete a drawing.
Time: 30-40 minutes
Setting: Classroom
Materials: Construction paper, crayons, markers
Procedure: Start by explaining that the activity is a cooperative drawing that needs to be completed without any talking. Have classmates choose their partners or bring together pairs as deemed necessary. Explain that partners will share a piece of paper and work together to complete a drawing. Students can select their own colored crayons or markers. Remember, partners are to complete the drawing without talking which means no prior communication as to what will be drawn. Talk about the types of nonverbal communication before beginning (hand signals, facial expressions, or other body language).

Follow-Up Discussion Questions

1. How did you feel when you wanted to talk to your partner and couldn't?
2. Did one of you take over while the other one sat by and just watched? How did that feel?
3. What do you think of your finished drawing?
4. How do you feel about your partner?

Mirror, Mirror

Goal: To make friends, and have a good time.
Time: 20 minutes
Setting: Classroom
Materials: None
Procedure: Have the children find a partner and instruct them to stand facing each other. Have the partners decide who will be partner A and who will be partner B. Tell the children that partner A is to move in any manner, the more ridiculous and outrageous the better. Partner A can make faces or do wild things with his or her body, but cannot move from where he or she is standing. Partner B is to act like a mirror, imitating every move partner A makes. It must be as though partner A were looking into a mirror. Have partner A start moving by playing some music, then freeze when the music stops. Try different types of music, because you'll be surprised what the variety of music does to the children's movement. After a few minutes of this have the partners switch roles so that partner B is the leader and partner A is the mirror. Some questions to ask for self-awareness afterward are:

• Which was the easier role for you, leader or follower?
• What is it like to be a leader?
• What is it like to be a follower?
• Are you a leader or a follower?

GA1501

Learning Appropriate Touch Activities

Touching and being held is our earliest source of self-awareness and healthy growth. We know that touching or hugging can help us to live longer, relieve depression and hypertension, strengthen the immune system, and improve family relations. Touching helps to significantly increase the amount of hemoglobin released into the blood stream. Hemoglobin is the protein matter inside of red blood cells that carries vital supplies of oxygen to all tissues of the body, especially the brain and heart. When considering the development of the human brain, new techniques show that touch is the prime source of neurochemical changes in infancy. When premature infants resting in incubators are massaged gently three times per day, they gain weight quicker and are released from the hospital faster than when "minimal touch" requirements are much lower.

Health is a very important subject area and component in the process of lifelong learning and enhancing self-esteem. Some general health objectives and skills to consider when addressing the issue of touch within the classroom are these: being able to tell the difference between good and bad touching, knowing what to do if someone touches a person in a way that feels uncomfortable, identifying touch as a way to protect yourself from disease, and identifying ways that families express love and respect for one another.

Sometimes teachers are reluctant to touch their students. "I don't touch the children," the teacher states. This is understandable especially when considering the increased occurrence of child abuse cases. No one wants to be accused of abusing a child. What we neglect to remember, however, is that touching is not a means to an end. Touching is an end in itself. Touching is meant to nurture and nourish, to express love and understanding.

The following cooperative games and activities will help children to experience appropriate touch while helping to create a sense of community. The activities are really just a bunch of fun, and by participating in these learning experiences, generally children begin to feel much more comfortable with touching. Some of the activities only require holding hands, and other activities call for actually giving hugs. Through these activities children also learn to strive for group goals.

GA1501

Booop!

Goal: Students will give their best effort towards realizing a group goal.
Time: 10 minutes
Setting: Room enough to move around freely
Materials: Balloons
Procedure: Have your students join hands in groups of six or more. The group has to keep the balloon in the air by batting the balloon with any part of their bodies, including hands, which must remain clasped. If the balloon touches the ground, the group loses the use of their hands to keep the balloon afloat. As the balloons eventually fall to the floor, continue to remove the parts of anatomy that the group is allowed to use to keep the balloon afloat, for example, elbows, shoulders, heads, thighs, etc. The group that eventually loses the use of their feet can begin the whole process again. Be careful of high kicks in a small circle.

Three-Corner Tag

Goal: Fast tag game using cooperative dodging skills and a fair amount of exercise.
Time: 10-20 minutes
Setting: Room enough to move around freely, the playground is best
Materials: None
Procedure: Form groups of four. Three of the four students hold hands in a circle or triangle while the fourth person stands outside of the triangle. The fourth person is the chaser. One person in the triangle volunteers to be the target. The three people in the triangle try to protect the target by moving and shifting. The target cannot be legally tagged on the arm or hand from across the triangle (no reaching in). For even more fun there can be triangles of four or five with more chasers.

Alligator!

Goal: Participants give their best effort to realize a group goal.
Time: 10 minutes
Setting: Playground
Materials: 2 to 3 playground benches that are approximately 10-16 feet (3-5 m) in length
Procedure: Place as many playground benches together (so that they are connected to make a longer bench) as needed for the size of your group. Have the children stand on top of the bench(es) in random order. On the command ALLIGATOR! the children are to readjust their line so that it is in order from the tallest to the shortest from one end to the other. If a student falls off the bench, he or she has automatically been eaten up by an alligator and, unfortunately, is out of the game for the time being. But don't worry; the next game of Alligator starts shortly!

GA1501

All Tied Up

Goal: Recreational activity to promote affiliation and cooperation.
Time: 5-10 minutes
Setting: Large enough space for members to form a circle
Materials: None
Procedure: A group with five to ten students are told to form a circle holding hands and then to tie themselves in knots by stepping over the clasped arms, around one another, over and under one another, etc. One group leader who has been standing outside of the circle facing away attempts to untie the knot. The person can untie the knot either physically, using his hands, or by giving verbal instructions. Sometimes it's not as easy as it sounds.

Sittin' in a Circle

Goal: Cooperation and giving one's best effort to realize a group goal.
Time: 10 minutes
Setting: Room enough to form a whole class circle
Materials: None
Procedure: Everyone in the classroom forms one circle with everyone facing in one direction. The circle should resemble a line of children where the first person has come full circle around to be behind the last person in line. The group will need to tighten up the circle so that there are no gaps, because each person is to sit in the lap of the person directly behind him or her. If the activity is successful, everyone will be sitting in the lap of another person. Then the group can actually start walking around in a circle while everyone is sitting in the lap of the other person. If the Sittin' Circle is unsuccessful, everyone falls on the ground, laughs, and starts over again. A good idea is to have everyone put his or her hands on the hips of the person in front and to count to three with everyone attempting to sit in the laps on three. Have fun!

GA1501

Hula-Hoop™ Roundup

Goal: Cooperation and giving one's best effort to realize a group goal.
Time: 30-40 minutes
Setting: Playground or gymnasium
Materials: Hula-Hoops™
Procedure: You will need one hula hoop for every two students to start this game. The Hula-Hoops™ provide a structure within which two or more children can play together. To start the game, have students pair off, with each pair standing inside a single Hula Hoop™. Each of the children within the Hula-Hoop™ is to hold up a portion of the hoop either at waist or shoulder level. Start playing music while each pair of children within the hoop skip, hop, jump, or walk around the room, staying inside of their hoop. In order for this to be successful, the two children must move in the same direction at the same pace. When the music stops, children from two different hoops team up together by stacking the hoops and getting inside of them. This sequence continues until as many children as possible are inside, holding up as many stacked hoops as possible. Most of the time about eight kids end up in one hoop (actually four hoops, all stacked on top of one another).

A variation of this game is when the Hula-Hoops™ are placed on the floor and the children skip, hop, jump, gallop, or perform animal walks around the room. When the music stops, the children jump inside the hoops on the floor. Each time the music stops, a Hula-Hoop™ is removed from the floor and all the children must work together to make sure that everyone, or a part of everyone, is inside the remaining hoops.

Everyone's Musical Chairs

Goal: Give one's best effort toward realizing a group goal.
Time: 30-40 minutes
Setting: Classroom or auditorium
Materials: 12-20 chairs, tape player and tape, or radio
Procedure: Unlike the typical way of playing Musical Chairs where children are eliminated if they don't find a chair to sit in when the music stops, in this cooperative game only the chairs are eliminated. The music stops and a chair is taken away and all the children must work together to sit, stand, or lie on the remaining chairs. The objective is to see how many chairs can be eliminated before the group finds it impossible to get up on the remaining chairs. This is a great cooperative game to watch, and it is interesting to observe how the children problem solve in order to get everyone on the remaining chairs.

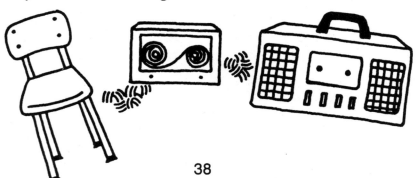

GA1501

Log Roll

Goal: To give one's best effort toward realizing a group goal, and to be comfortable with touching another student.

Time: 20-30 minutes

Setting: Gymnasium or grassy area

Materials: Tumbling mats

Procedure: A group of children lie side by side together on their stomachs on a mat, rug, grass, or any other soft surface. A child who is the "rider" will lie on his or her stomach perpendicular to the children (logs), across the upper part of their backs. All the children logs then begin log rolling in the same direction, allowing the rider on their backs a somewhat bumpy but cuddly ride across the top. Once the top rider has been rolled over the last log, he or she then becomes a rolling log at the end of the line of logs. The first child log at the beginning of the line of logs then becomes the next rider to go over the top of the other logs. This continues until the line of logs runs out of space or until everyone feels like stopping.

Caterpillar

Goal: Students will be able to play together cooperatively to promote affiliation and group cohesion.

Time: 20-30 minutes

Setting: Gymnasium or grassy field

Materials: Tumbling mats, rug or grassy surface (soft surface)

Procedure: Using a soft surface (rug, tumbling mats, grassy area) have all the children lie down on their stomachs side by side. Make sure all the kids are lying tightly together; there should be no gaps. Next have the student at the very end of the line roll, like a log, over onto his neighbor and continue rolling down the row of children's bodies until he reaches the end. This child should then lie down on his stomach while the next person at the other end begins rolling in the very same manner until everyone has rolled over the top of everyone else. Once the caterpillar gets "crawling" you'll find that they can travel the whole length of a grassy field. Sometimes it's really great to have two caterpillars going at the same time. Race time!

GA1501

Rag Dolls and Tin Soldiers

Goal: Students will be able to work with a partner cooperatively and creatively, utilizing touch in a goal-directed way.

Time: 30 minutes

Setting: Classroom, outside, or gymnasium

Materials: None

Procedure: Have each child pair up with someone approximately the same size. When all have found partners, have the children decide who will be partner A and who will be partner B. Tell them that the A's will be the tin soldiers and the B's will be the master. Tell them that the tin soldiers are toys and they have no brains, so they can only move forward. Ask the children if any of them knows how a tin soldier walks. Then have a child who knows demonstrate. Make sure the soldiers walk with stiff arms and legs. B's job is to guide his tin soldier around the room and to prevent the soldier from walking into any obstacles. Sometimes things can get a little outrageous with this activity, so keep an eye out for inappropriate behavior. After a few minutes stop the tin soldiers and the masters and have them switch roles.

Now partner A is to lie on his or her back on the ground. Partner A is going to become the rag doll. Rag dolls are completely limp (just the opposite of tin soldiers). Rag dolls cannot move. Partner B's job is to try to stand the rag doll up. This can be a lot of fun because if the rag doll remains completely limp it's almost impossible to stand it up. After a few minutes of this have the partners switch roles. What a great time!

The Human Machine

Goal: The whole class will work together cooperatively to play the role of a fast-moving machine.

Time: 30 minutes

Setting: Classroom

Materials: None

Procedure: In this activity all the students in the classroom will work together to form a machine using their bodies. Each student will become a moving part of the machine so that each is attached to at least two other parts. Have the class stand in a circle and ask them to think of all the parts of a machine they could become (rods, pulleys, screws, wheels, etc.). Find one volunteer to begin by making a machinelike movement in the center of the group. When that person has the movement down and has developed a rhythm, add another student to the machine. That student should become a part of the machine by connecting to a "part" that is already moving (another student). Have the rest of the class connect to manufacture a whole class human machine.

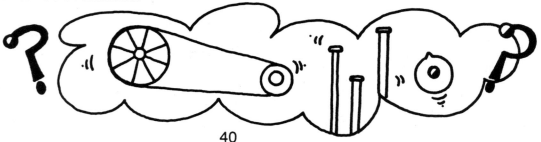

GA1501

Bear Backs

Goal: Students will develop a sense of fellowship with other students.
Time: 5 minutes
Setting: Classroom
Materials: None
Procedure: Have your children stand up near their chairs in the classroom. Have them find a partner and tell them to stand back to back with each other. Ask them, "Have you ever been to the zoo?" "Have you ever watched a bear scratch his back up against a tree?" Then say, "Pretend that you are a bear and your back really needs a good scratching. You and your partner are both bears, but you don't have a tree to scratch against so you'll just have to scratch up against each other!" Scratch, scratch, scratch!

Hug Tag

Goal: Students will be able to work together cooperatively to find gentle and peaceful solutions to problems or challenges.
Time: 30 minutes
Setting: Playground or gymnasium
Materials: None
Procedure: This is a tag game that you can play by whatever rules you are used to in tag games. However, the major exception to this specific way of playing is that the only time a player is safe is when he or she is hugging another player. After playing for a while with only two-person hugs, change the rules so that in order to be safe, three players must be hugging. Then increase the number to four and then to five. This game is lots of great fun!

GA1501

"Buddy" Activities

Have your students pair up with a "buddy" and try some of these friendship-building activities!

Buddy Balloon Balance

In this game one balloon is to be shared by two children. The two children will work together to discover different ways to hold the balloon between their bodies without using their hands. They can hold hands, but they cannot touch the balloon. The children attempt to move around the classroom while continuing to hold the balloon between themselves in different ways. Perhaps the children can be given the challenge of trying to move through an obstacle course of chairs, desks, Hula-Hoops™, benches, etc.

Buddy Pull-Up

Buddies sit down on the floor facing each other. Their feet must be flat on the floor, with their knees bent and their toes touching each other's. The buddies then reach forward clasping hands and, by pulling together, both rise to a standing position. The buddies can then return to the sitting position. The children are given the opportunity to do this repeatedly if they wish. It's great for building upper body strength, which most children desperately need. This activity can also be done with more than two people. Usually a group of 4, 6, or 8 is best–even numbers. The children sit in a circle with their feet in the center. Everyone grabs another person's hand and the whole group tries to pull itself up to the standing position.

Buddy Back-Up

Buddies sit back to back, with their knees bent and their feet flat on the ground. The children interlock their arms at the elbows and then try to stand up by pushing against the other's back without moving their feet. Then the children can sit down and try it again. The teacher must mention that in order to do this successfully the children are not allowed to put their hands on the ground. They can only use the force of their buddies to help them get off the ground. This activity can also be attempted in larger groups. Again, groups of 4, 6, or 8 are best.

Buddy Handshake

Buddies stand facing each other and grab right hands as if shaking hands. Buddy number 1 swings his or her right leg over the head and arm of Buddy number 2, so that the legs take a straddling position over the clasped arms. Buddy number 2 then swings his or her left leg over Buddy number 1 so that the buddies are now standing buttocks to buttocks, while still holding hands. Then Buddy number 1 continues by bringing his or her left leg over the clasped arms so he or she faces in the original position. Buddy number 2 swings his or her right leg over the clasped arms so he or she also returns to the original position.

Buddy Hop

Buddies stand facing each other and both raise their right legs straight out from the hip, high enough so that the partner can hold the ankle in his or her left hand. When the buddies are able to balance with both of them standing on one leg holding their partner's leg by the ankle in their right hand, they can try to hop along, around in a circle or wherever. For a very difficult stunt, the buddies may try to lower themselves to the floor while continuing to stand on one leg only, and then return to the standing position once again.

GA1501

Fun and Fitness Challenge Activities

I challenge you to try these four activities with your class. Just make up four teams, decide on four "monitors" to record the points for each team at each station, hand out the score sheets to the team captains, make sure the station monitors record their teams' points, and have a great time!

Target Practice: Kick and Throw

Children line up on one side of a handball court. Have them line up behind the farthest line of the playing area. Each child will be given three attempts to kick a ball at a square target (taped off area on the wall). Each time the kicked ball hits the target, a point will be scored for the team. Next the children line up on the other side of the handball wall. They will now be given three attempts to throw various types of balls into a large target (perhaps a clean fifty-gallon garbage can). Each time a ball makes it into the target, a point will be scored for the team. Depending on how many children are on the team, the facilitator may wish to have the children perform each activity twice.

"Grid"

Lines must be taped on, or drawn on with chalk, so that a grid of squares will be placed on the ground. The individual squares should have dimensions of $1^1/_2$' x $1^1/_2$' (45.72 x 45.72 cm). The squares should be designed so that you have overall dimensions of five squares wide by six or seven squares long. Each row or level of squares should have one square crossed off so that the children will only be allowed to step into that one square. The children should proceed through the grid until they make it successfully to the other side or until they step into the wrong square. If they make it successfully to the other side by stepping into all the correct squares, score a point for the team. If the child steps into the wrong square, he or she has to go to the end of the line to try again. The facilitator should have two grids with different squares crossed off in case the whole team makes it through the first grid successfully. *Children will not know where the *X*s are. They will have to find out through trial and error.

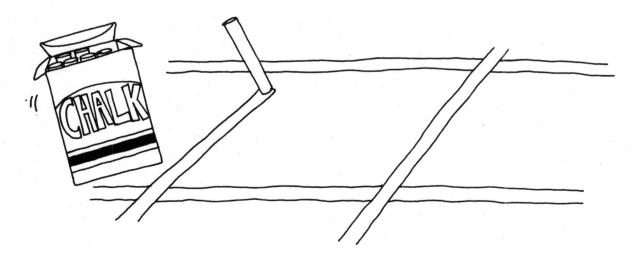

Quicksand Crossing

Children will attempt to have their whole team make it across a quicksand river without touching the ground. One point is scored for each child who makes it across successfully. Each team will be given two boards (2" x 6" [5.08 x 15.24 cm]) approximately 6 feet (1.82 m) in length, and five to eight large-sized coffee cans. The team must work together cooperatively, using the boards and cans, to make it across to the other side. If a child steps on the ground (even if it's with only one foot) he or she perishes in the quicksand. The boards must not touch the ground because they, too, will sink into the quicksand. The only items that do not sink are the tin cans. Children use the tin cans as platforms to place the boards on to construct a bridge across the quicksand river. If a whole team makes it across, score three bonus points. If there is still time remaining, have the team try to make it back to the original side, but this time take away one or two of the tin cans. Make sure the quicksand river is approximately twice as long as the length of the two boards.

Relay Races

An obstacle course of chairs or cones must be laid out for the children to zigzag around. Use from five to ten chairs or cones. For the first relay use a tennis ball or small ball. Facilitator places the ball between the elbows of the first person. This person must run with the ball between his or her elbows in zigzag fashion around the obstacles. Upon returning to the line he or she must give the ball to the next person in line with both participants using their elbows only. No hands! For the second relay, two children must work together. Using a large playground ball placed between them, the children stand back to back. With the ball between them, no hands are used as the partners proceed through the same obstacle course. If the ball falls from between their backs they can either pick the ball up and place it back between them, or go to the end of the line to try again later. Points are scored each time a pair of children makes it across the finish line.

All points are tallied and winning teams receive a prize. Actually all the children are winners simply because they participated and gave their best effort, so give a prize to everyone. YEAH!

44

Fun and Fitness Challenge Score Sheet

Team Number: _____

Activity	Points	Initials
1. Target Practice: Kick and Throw	_____	_____
2. "Grid"	_____	_____
3. Quicksand Crossing	_____	_____
4. Relay Races	_____	_____
Total Points	_____	

GA1501

Journal Writing for Creating a Sense of Community

If you have been incorporating journal-writing activities in your classroom instruction, by now your students probably know what time of day they will be writing. My guess is that by now they look forward to journal-writing time. Now you might want to try a new idea in journal writing. Ask your students if they would like to write in one of their fellow classmate's journals. Some of the sentence stems provided make for great "note passing" opportunities. To get started, just write one of these community-creating sentence stems on the board and invite the children to do the rest. For the "note-passing" opportunities, allow time for journal exchange. Make sure you explain that in order for there to be a journal exchange, both persons must agree to the exchange.

- When I'm with my friends we . . .

- My friends help me to . . .

- I make new friends by . . .

- When I'm on a team I . . .

- I make others feel wanted by . . .

- I like to be around friends when . . .

- When I help my classmates learn I . . .

- My favorite partner is _____ because . . .

- My friends like me because . . .

- I wish people would stop . . .

- If I were in charge of the world, I would have people . . .

- To help a person feel like he or she belongs, I must . . .

- The best part about my family is . . .

- If someone is different from me, I . . .

- To be a good team, our class must . . .

- You are a special friend because . . .

- To be happy with my friends I . . .

- I can help others by . . .

- To be a good friend, one must . . .

- A friend is . . .

- I help others feel important by . . .

- Being a good classmate means . . .

- The best part about our class is . . .

- When I play a game with others I . . .

- When other classmates help me I . . .

- _____ is a good buddy to me because . . .

- I like to give . . .

- I would like to know _____ better because . . .

- If I could invite all my friends to do anything that I wanted, we would . . .

- The world would be a better place if everyone would . . .

- To live in peace, people must . . .

- When I argue with someone, I feel . . .

- The best thing about my friend _____ is . . .

- When someone that I like likes me too, I feel . . .

- I like to be around people who . . .

- I like to listen to other people tell me . . .

Interdisciplinary Activities

Visual Arts

Friendly Webs

Goal: Using art elements and principles, students will be able to express affirming feelings towards others.

Time: Approximately 1 hour

Setting: Classroom or art room

Materials: White construction paper, pencils, crayons, watercolors, paintbrushes, water containers, paper towels

Procedure: In our story Charlotte spins a web with words that describe special traits and characteristics of Wilbur. This activity will give your students an opportunity to create a colorful web where they will write positive and affirming words describing fellow classmates. Before starting you'll want to begin with a discussion that will enable your students to think of positive words that they will use to describe a friend in the classroom. Ask, "Who can remember the wonderful words that Charlotte used to describe Wilbur?" "What kinds of words would you use to describe positive things about your friends here in this room?" Write their answers on the board. Now your students have enough words to use and you're ready to begin the art project.

Begin the art project by distributing 11" x 17" (27.97 x 43.18 cm) pieces of white construction paper. Then have your students use pencils to draw their webs. Drawing the webs first with pencil will allow the inevitable mistakes to be corrected. The web is created by first drawing a point near the middle of the paper. This point will be the focal point where the web's foundation lines will emanate. After seven lines have been drawn emanating from the focal point extending all the way to the edge, have your children draw the connecting lines to the web. This is done by drawing lines that start near the focal point and spiral continuously outward as far as paper space will permit. The lines should "swoop" as they would in a natural spider's web, as they connect to the foundation lines. After the web has been drawn in pencil have your students trace the web with their crayons. Make sure they press hard to make their lines thick. Once the lines have been traced with crayons, have your students write the affirming word describing their friend within the web. Make sure those words are heavily traced with a crayon as well. Finally, the whole paper can be covered with watercolors. Children can paint the whole paper the same color, or they can use as many colors as they wish. The wax from the crayon web will prevent the various colors from washing into one another. When completed, hang up all the colorful new webs throughout your classroom or have your students present their art projects to their friends!

GA1501

Science

Spider Specifics

Goal: Students will understand that spiders are unique animals that are to be valued and respected.

Time: Several days

Setting: Classroom

Materials: Pencil, paper, markers, crayons, poster board

Procedure: How much do you know about spiders? Do you know what kind of spider Charlotte was? What do spiders eat? How many legs do spiders have? How many eyes do spiders have? What is the largest part of a spider's face? How many body parts does a spider have? Do spiders have hair? What are some of the different types of webs that spiders spin? Do spiders fly? What are some famous spiders?

Take your class on a spider hunt and see what you can find. If you can catch a spider, take it back and keep it in a glass jar for a few days of observation. Put a little soil on the bottom, add a few leaves and twigs, punch a few small holes in the lid, and you'll have an effective spider cage. While your class is observing the spider have them write a report or make a poster on the following "Spider Specifics":

Charlotte: Grey spider

Spider Food: Spiders eat flies, beetles, grasshoppers, gnats, butterflies, centipedes, mosquitoes, crickets, midges, moths, etc.

Legs: All spiders have eight legs with seven segments each.

Eyes: Most spiders have eight eyes, but some have six, and a few have only two.

Face: The largest part of a spider's face is its pair of jaws. Spiders use their jaws to capture and poison insects.

Body Parts: All spiders have three body parts: the head, thorax, and abdomen.

Hair: A spider's body is covered by thousands of hairs that are used as an important sensory organ.

Webs: Different kinds of spiders make differently shaped webs. Here are some of the types: funnel, sheet, and orb (round).

Flight: A baby spider, called a spiderling, flies with the use of long silk threads coming from its spinneret.

Famous Spiders: Tarantula, black widow, and trap-door spider

48

GA1501

Social Science

Farm Animals

Goal: Students will understand how people are dependent upon the resources that farm animals provide.

Time: Several days

Setting: Classroom

Materials: Pencils, paper, markers, crayons, poster board

Procedure: Farming is perhaps the most important job in the world. People cannot live without the food that farms provide. In *Charlotte's Web* the Zuckerman farm was a family farm where there were many different kinds of animals. These animals provide food, friendship, and help to humans. Without these domesticated animals life would be very difficult. Have your students develop a chart telling how humans depend on farm animals for many different resources. As your students research, incorporate the use of *Charlotte's Web* as well as other resources in the construction of the chart.

Farm Animals	How They Help Humans
Goats and Dairy Cows	Milk, cheese, and butter
Beef Cattle, Pigs, and Sheep	Meat (beef, pork, and lamb)
Chickens, Ducks, Geese, and Turkeys	Eggs and meat (poultry)
Dogs	Herd and guard cattle and sheep
Horses	Transportation, hauling supplies, plowing
Cats	Keep away mice

GA1501

What Is a Friend? [1]

A friend is someone who is concerned with
everything you do
A friend is someone to call upon during good
and bad times
A friend is someone who understands
whatever you do
A friend is someone who tells you the truth
about yourself
A friend is someone who knows what you are
going through at all times
A friend is someone who does not compete
with you
A friend is someone who is genuinely happy
for you when things go well
A friend is someone who tries to cheer you up
when things don't go well
A friend is an extension of yourself without
which you are not complete
THANK YOU FOR BEING MY FRIEND

Susan Polis Schultz

Was Charlotte Wilbur's friend?
What did Charlotte do that made her an excellent friend?

_____

_____

_____

_____

_____

_____

_____

---

1. From the book: *The Speaker's Sourcebook* by Glenn Van Ekeren, 1988. Used by permission of the publisher, Prentice Hall/A Division of Simon & Schuster, Englewood Cliffs, NJ.

Everybody Together

Fern, Wilbur, Charlotte, Templeton, Gander, Goose, the Goslings, the Sheep, the Lambs, Mr. and Mrs. Arable, Avery, Mr. and Mrs. Zuckerman, Lurvy, and Dr. Dorian were all friendly.

What sort of words make up friendship?
Write a word for each letter.

F _____

R _____

I _____

E _____

N _____

D _____

S _____

H _____

I _____

P _____

GA1501

Me and My Friends

In the Zuckerman's barn all the animals become good friends. Everyone likes to have friends. Answer these questions about you and your friends.

When I'm at school, my friends and I _____

_____

When I'm with a friend, I feel _____

_____

When I'm at recess, my friends and I _____

_____

When a friend feels sad, I _____

_____

When I'm with a friend, our favorite thing to do is _____

_____

When I'm being a good friend, I _____

_____

When my friend has a problem, I usually _____

_____

The qualities I look for in a friend are _____

_____

The things I do to make new friends are _____

_____

I'm happiest with my friends when we _____

_____

Miracles!

To help save Wilbur's life Charlotte performed a miracle. She wrote words in her web describing Wilbur. Wilbur didn't believe those things about himself before Charlotte wrote them. But as soon as Charlotte wrote the words Wilbur became . . .

Pretend that you have a very special friend who is going to write special miracle words about you. Write the miracle words in the webs below. Do you believe in miracles?

GA1501

A Place to Belong

Because of Charlotte, Wilbur had a place where he felt at home. The barn was Wilbur's place to belong. He was never without friends. Charlotte's children and grandchildren lived in the doorway year after year. And people visited Wilbur all the time because they never forgot the year of the miracle. The barn was happy, safe, and secure.

Everyone needs a place to belong. We all need to feel wanted and respected. We all want to feel accepted. Everybody wants to have friends. How can you help to make your classroom a place to belong?

_____

_____

_____

Draw a picture of your classroom as a place to belong. What does it look like? What does it feel like? Is everyone smiling? What is everyone doing? Do you like being there?

GA1501

Name: _____   Date: _____

Find a Friend!

Find a friend who:

1. speaks two languages _____

2. is an only child _____

3. has a computer _____

4. wears the same size shoe as you do _____

5. has an older sister _____

6. was born the same month as you _____

7. knows how to ski_____

8. can whistle through his or her fingers_____

9. has been backpacking _____

10. is the youngest in the family _____

11. has a dog _____

12. is about the same height as you_____

13. can play a musical instrument_____

14. has a collection of some kind _____

15. loves to read _____

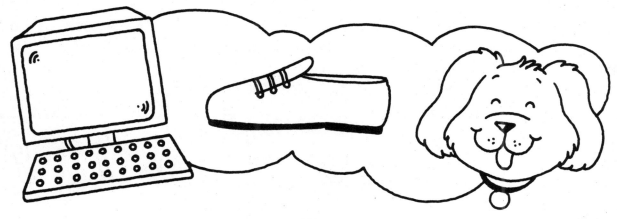

GA1501

Community Certificate

This certificate is awarded to _____ for being the type of classmate who helps others to feel valued and important. In being a good buddy you have helped to make our classroom feel like a real community where we all belong.

This certificate will help to show others that _____ is a great team member who works well with others to reach all team goals.

Congratulations,

_____!

Awarded on the _____ day of _____

Signed: _____
(teacher)

56

GA1501

Developing Self-Awareness

"Do not wish to be anything but what you are, and try to be that perfectly."
— St. Francis de Sales

The Inner Picture of Self-Concept and Self-Image

With the help of caring, respectful friends we are affiliated with, we can begin to develop self-awareness. Self-awareness is comprised of both self-concept and self-image. Self-concept is an objective description of our physical appearance, abilities, values, behavior, and thoughts. Self-image is the visual representation of our self that we hold within our mind. When we close our eyes and imagine ourselves, we are bringing to mind our self-image. It is important to understand that we do not attach a value judgment to our self-concept or self-image. Our job is to help students develop accurate self-awareness. Accurate self-awareness is critical to building self-esteem because it will form the foundation of self-evaluation.

Developing Self-Awareness with *Crow Boy*

In this wonderfully sensitive story about a forlorn little tagalong nicknamed Chibi, meaning "tiny boy," Taro Yashima shows us how helping a child to become aware of his uniqueness can be a life-changing event.

In the very beginning of the story Chibi is shown hidden away in the dark space below the schoolhouse, afraid of the other children and the teacher. Once inside the classroom Chibi is very removed from all the other children. Always left alone, always at the end of the line, always at the foot of the class, little Chibi finds an ever increasing number of ways to keep himself isolated. Soon the other children begin to pick on him and call him names.

The years go by with Chibi going to school faithfully every day until the sixth grade, when a kind, new teacher arrives. The new teacher takes an interest in Chibi and discovers all the unique qualities of this isolated little boy. We discover how much Chibi knows about plants and flowers. We see how the teacher tacks up on the wall Chibi's drawings and unique handwriting that no one else can read. And then one day the school has a talent show, and who should appear on stage but the "stupid" little boy, nicknamed Chibi. The teacher announces, much to the shock of the audience, that Chibi is going to imitate the voices of crows. And with this unique talent, Chibi takes the children to that faraway and lonely place where he lives with his family. Soon every one of the children begins to cry, thinking of all the times that they had been cruel to this different and unique little boy.

Graduation day comes, and Chibi is the only student given an award for perfect attendance through all six years. No longer does anyone call him Chibi; now when he comes to town everyone calls him by his new name–Crow Boy. And he wears this unique name proudly as he completes his chores in the village.

"Crow Boy would nod and smile as if he liked the name. And when his work was done he would buy a few things for his family. Then he would set off for his home on the far side of the mountain, stretching his growing shoulders proudly like a grown-up man. And from around the turn of the mountain road would come a crow call—the happy one." [1]

Take the time to find out what is unique about the students in your classroom. Help them to become aware of their abilities, feelings, and culture. Watch them shine as they begin to learn about their special characteristics.

Thematic Unit:	Self-Awareness
Core Literature:	*Crow Boy* by Taro Yashima (Puffin Books)
Extended Literature:	*Feelings* by Aliki (Greenwillow Books)
	People by Peter Spier (Doubleday)

Additional Literature Supporting the Theme of Self-Awareness

Frederick by Leo Lionni (Knopf Books for Young Readers)
A Gathering of Days: A New England Girl's Journal by Joan Blos (Macmillan Children's Book Group)
Gilberto and the Wind by Marie Hall Ets (Viking Children's Books)
Harold and the Purple Crayon by Crockett Johnson (HarperCollins Children's Books)
Harry the Dirty Dog by Gene Zion (HarperCollins Children's Books)
Hats, Hats, Hats by Ann Morris (Lothrop, Lee & Shepard Books)
Higher on the Door by James Stevenson (Greenwillow Books)
House of Dies Drear by Virginia Hamilton (Macmillan Children's Book Group)
How Do I Feel? by Norma Simon (Albert Whitman & Co.)
The Hundred Penny Box by Sharon Bell Mathis (Puffin Books)
I Like to Be Me by Barbara Bel Geddes (Young Readers Press)
Imogene's Antlers by David Small (Crown Books for Young Readers)
I'm Terrific by Marjorie Weinman Sharmat (Holiday House, Inc.)
I Wish I Were a Butterfly by James Howe (Harcourt Brace & Co.)
Jambo Means Hello: Swahili Alphabet Book by Muriel Feelings (Dial Books for Young Readers)
The Kids' Book of Questions by Gregory Stock (Workman Publications)
Knots on a Counting Rope by Bill Martin, Jr. and John Archambault (Henry Holt & Co.)
Millions of Cats by Wanda Gag (Putnam Publishing)
Mysteries of Harris Burdick by Chris Van Allsburg (Houghton Mifflin)
Not So Fast, Songololo by Niki Daly (Macmillan Children's Book Group)
Phantom Tollbooth by Norton Juster (Knopf Books for Young Readers)
Pinkerton, Behave by Steven Kellogg (Dial Books for Young Readers)
Sam, Bangs and Moonshine by Evaline Ness (Henry Holt & Co.)
Someday by Charlotte Zolotow (HarperCollins Children's Books)
The Tale of Peter Rabbit by Beatrix Potter (Frederick Wayne & Co., Inc.)
There's a Nightmare in My Closet by Mercer Mayer (Puffin Books)
The Three Bears by Paul Galdone (Clarion Books/Tickner & Fields)
Tikki Tikki Tembo by Arlene Mosel (Henry Holt & Co.)
The Whingdingdilly by Bill Peet (Houghton Mifflin)
Why Am I Different? by Norma Simon (Albert Whitman & Co.)

---

1. From CROW BOY by Taro Yashima. Copyright © 1955 by Mitsu and Taro Yashima, renewed 1983 by Mitsu and Taro Yashima. Used by permission of Viking Penguin, a division of Penguin Books USA Inc.

GA1501

Supporting Subthemes of Self-Awareness

The following subthemes help to support or complement developing self-awareness, the third step of enhancing self-esteem. Subthemes provide a tangent for either the teacher or the students to take when developing understanding of the theme of self-awareness.

- Beauty
- Being
- Culture
- Heritage
- Emotions
- Evolution
- Happiness
- Values

- Ideas
- Knowledge
- Race
- Mental Health
- Mind
- Physical Health
- Senses
- Love

- Skills
- Behavior
- People
- Thoughts
- Dreams
- Abilities
- Virtue

Self-Esteem Theme Objectives

The teacher will . . .

1. **Provide opportunities to discover thoughts, values, abilities, and physical attributes.** Together all of these characteristics determine our personalities. All people have special qualities that make them special or unique. We are born with some of these special characteristics and qualities, and others develop as we grow and mature. Try the "Me and My Personality" activity to help students improve their self-concept and self-image.

2. **Improve students' abilities to identify and appropriately express their feelings.** Individuals are exactly who they think they are, and they express emotions that are based upon their thoughts and attitudes. When children are able to express their emotions, they have a better understanding of themselves. When children understand the thoughts behind the emotions, they learn to respond to events in a more productive manner–enhancing their self-esteem.

3. **Promote positive thinking through affirming declarations.** Affirming declarations are positive thoughts that develop our beliefs and feelings. Positive thoughts help people to feel positively of themselves and respond to events in a productive manner.

4. **Facilitate the awareness of influential models on the self.** We learn who we are based upon where we come from, who we live with, and the activities we perform. Family, friends, teachers, television, radio, books, and other mediums all influence our behavior and the way we describe ourselves. Think about it. Are you surrounding yourself with the correct influences to enhance your self-esteem?

5. **Identify individual heritage, race, and culture.** We have become a multicultural society with a significant amount of human variety and difference in the world. By providing opportunities and lessons that challenge the assumptions and beliefs that we have about these differences, students will learn to respect, understand, and value all of humankind. We are all together in this race, the human race.

The students will . . .

- Acquire a feeling of individuality and specialness.
- Develop self-knowledge which includes an accurate and realistic description of their background, roles, attributes, and beliefs.
- Become aware of their feelings while learning how to express them assertively.

GA1501

Interpersonal Activities

Who Am I ?

Goal: Students will be able to describe positive characteristics, personality traits, and abilities.

Time: 30-40 minutes

Setting: Classroom

Materials: Paper and pencils

Procedure: For this activity have your students complete twenty statements of "Who am I?" This may take some time, so allow about fifteen minutes. Once finished you may want to have your students exchange their papers or you may gather all the papers to be read aloud to the group. Have one student read the statements written without revealing the name while the others try to guess who the author is. Or the written statements may be kept by owners and disclosed to one other student of their choosing.

Variation: Students may pair off with another partner and sit facing each other with knees almost touching. One person is to ask the other "Who are you?" in rapid succession while the other continues to respond for 60-90 seconds. The person responding has to say something each time the question is asked, even if he or she cannot come up with another response. Participants are asked to notice how they respond. Do their responses address the words *be*, *do*, or *have*? You may want to ask, "Why do you get stuck and what is the answer you get 'stuck' with?"

What's in the Bag?

Goal: Students will be able to identify their dreams and desires.

Time: 50-60 minutes

Setting: Classroom

Materials: Paper bags, magazines, newspapers, scissors, glue

Procedure: Children search through magazines and newspapers to find pictures and statements that represent themselves at this time in their lives. These pictures are of things that they are willing to let others know about them. Give each person a paper bag and instruct everyone to paste these pictures on the outside of the bag. Next, the children search through magazines and newspapers for pictures and statements of the things they dream of having, doing, or becoming later in life. Instruct the students to put these things inside their bags. Each child shares with the class about the pictures and statements inside and outside of the bag. Save the bags until the end of the year when the students will look inside and evaluate if they have come any closer to realizing their dreams and desires of who and what they want to have, do, or be. Explain that each of us has the potential "inside" of ourselves to become whatever we desire.

Variation: Have the students put pictures and statements inside the bag which represent those qualities and experiences which they hide from others. Discussion may focus on the "face" we present to the outside world and how accurately it is perceived by others; discussion may include sharing of "inner selves" as well. Sometimes it is best not to require, or even ask, students to share their "inner bag selves."

GA1501

Pride Line

Goal: Describe ways to be proud of oneself and others.

Time: 10 minutes

Setting: The classroom while lining up

Materials: None

Procedure: Before lining up, each child is to share one thing to be proud of. For some children this may be very difficult. Explain that pride is a feeling of self-esteem arising from one's accomplishments, possessions, attributes, etc. Other children may help the ones having difficulty by suggesting something to be proud of. The most important element is to get everyone to express at least one thing to be proud of. The more you include this experiential element in your class, the more the class looks forward to it, and the more they learn that they have much to be proud of. Be patient and remember that eventually it gets easier for the children to think of something to be proud of. Try constructing a bulletin board with this title and acronym for the word *Pride* displayed above your students' successfully completed work.

"Work We Take Pride In"
PRIDE = Personal Responsibility In Daily Effort.

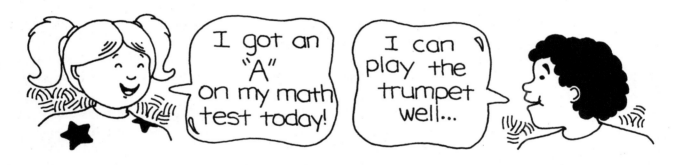

Incognito

Goal: Students will be able to express personal feelings in order to increase self-awareness and develop empathy for others.

Time: 20-30 minutes

Setting: Classroom

Materials: Masking tape, paper, pencils

Procedure: Form groups of six to twelve students in order for them to solve the dilemma of agreeing upon the ten most important things to take on a trip to the moon. Before beginning, however, assign each student a role that will dictate how the other group members will interact with him or her. Write the roles on masking tape or adhesive name tags and place them on each student's forehead so he or she won't know what role he or she has. Some great ideas for roles are Insult Me, Ignore Me, Encourage Me, Respect Me, Fear Me, Laugh at Me, etc. You may want to assign roles that relate to the students to develop more empathy towards the way they treat others. For example, if you have a student who is always laughing and poking fun at others, you may want to place the "Laugh at Me" role on his or her head. Afterward promote a discussion on how it feels to be treated in certain ways.

GA1501

Me and My Personality

Goal: Students will be able to identify the elements that comprise their personalities thus improving their self-concept.

Time: Several days

Setting: Classroom and large space with no desks and chairs

Materials: Large sheet of butcher paper for each child, pencils, markers, crayons, work sheet entitled "Me and My Personality" on page 65.

Procedure:
1. Start by saying, "Each of us has certain characteristics that make us special and unique. We are born with special characteristics and qualities, and we also develop other characteristics and qualities as we get older."

2. Write the word *personality* on the chalkboard and then ask your students, "What do you think your personality is?" After they respond tell them, "Each of you has your own unique personality, and your personality is everything about you."

3. Tell them, "Your personality is made up of your traits and appearance, abilities and skills, thoughts and feelings, and also your values and actions."

4. Explain that:

   "Your *traits and appearance* include things such as the way you look, how tall you are, what kind of body you have, the color of your hair, eyes, and skin. It also includes how you take care of the way you look. In other words, your grooming habits–how you comb your hair or keep yourself clean.

   "Your *abilities and skills* include the things that you can do well. These are the special talents or capabilities that you have, such as being good at dancing, singing, reading, writing, sports, or drawing.

   "Your *thoughts and feelings* include the things you like or dislike. These are your opinions and beliefs. They also include your emotions, such as happy, sad, angry, afraid, or confused.

   "Your *values* are the things you think are important. They are the rules that you live by and the feelings that influence the way you behave and what you do. And your *actions* are those things you do. Your actions are guided by your values. For example if you value good music, you will take action or do things such as spending your money on records or tapes. Or if you like, or value, or think it is important to have fun with friends, you might take action or do things like going to Disneyland or to the park."

5. Next disclose to your students, "Some things that are valuable or important to me are . . ." Examples might include family, friends, money, college degree and teaching certificate, food, health, honesty, and so on.

GA1501

6. Then ask the class, "What are the different things, behaviors, or ideals that are important to you?" Write their answers on the chalkboard.

7. Ask them, "Now look carefully at the list of values on the board and decide which ones are the most important to you. Raise your hand if _____ is important to you. Raise your hand if _____ is important to you." Count the number of hands raised for each value and put the number next to the word on the board. (Perhaps you will want the students to construct a bar graph of each of the values and the number of responses for those values.)

8. To conclude this lesson, ask a few questions such as "How do we get our values?" "How do our values influence the things that we do?"

9. Next pass out the "Me and My Personality" work sheet and have the students fill in their answers for each of the different areas of their personality. After the students have had an opportunity to complete the assignment, discuss their answers. Tell the students to hold onto the work sheet because it will be used later for a special project.

10. After completion of the work sheet ask the students to help one another trace outlines of their bodies onto life-sized art utility sheets or butcher paper. Then have them write their personality characteristics around their body outlines and draw or paint or color what they believe they look like within the outline.

Note: This exercise could be accompanied with a science lesson on anatomy. Instead of drawing their outer portraits, the students could draw different systems of their internal body, such as skeletal system, muscular system, circulatory system, digestive system, etc.

GA1501

Me and My Personality

Thoughts and Feelings

I feel good about myself.

I like my dog.

Abilities and Skills

I can kick a football.

I can sing

Traits and Appearance

I have black hair.

I have brown skin.

Values and Actions

I like honest people.

I study hard to be smart.

GA1501

Me and My Personality Work Sheet

My Thoughts and Feelings: List what you believe, your opinions and feelings, what you like and don't like.

_____

_____

_____

My Abilities and Skills: List your special talents, the sports you play well, what you do well at school, your special hobbies.

_____

_____

_____

My Traits and Appearance: Describe the way you look, how you dress, the color of your hair and eyes.

_____

_____

_____

My Values and Actions: Describe how you feel about family, things, and friendship. Also describe your standards, rules, or ideals.

_____

_____

_____

GA1501

"I Am Unique!" Poem

Goal: Students will become more aware of their special characteristics, dreams, and desires.

Time: Several days

Setting: Classroom

Materials: Construction paper, pencil, crayons, markers, book-binding materials

Procedure: Write the following poem on the board or provide a copy to each student. Read over the poem and fill in responses for yourself to provide an example for your students. Then have your students construct individual books by filling in their own responses to the sentences. Have them write their poems on pieces of paper. Then they may construct their books by drawing illustrations to coincide with some of the responses they gave. Have them devote two full pages for each stanza, with the words on one page and the illustration on the other.

1st Stanza

I am (list two special characteristics you have)
I wonder (something that you are curious about)
I hear (an imaginary sound you would like to hear)
I see (an imaginary sight you would like to see)
I want (something you really want to have)
I am (repeat the first line of this stanza)

2nd Stanza

I pretend (write something you actually pretend to do)
I feel (write a feeling that you sometimes have)
I touch (something you can imagine touching)
I worry (something that really troubles you)
I cry (something that makes you very sad)
I am (repeat the first line of the poem)

3rd Stanza

I understand (write something you know is true)
I say (something you believe in)
I dream (something you actually dream about)
I try (something you try really hard to do)
I hope (something you actually hope for)
I am (repeat the first line of the poem)

GA1501

We Become What We Think About

Our brains work amazingly fast. On the average we think between 10,000 and 50,000 thoughts per day. That means that we're generating about 1000 to 5000 thoughts per hour. Many of these thoughts are actually about ourselves. So one has to wonder if these thoughts are self-promoting thoughts or self-limiting thoughts.

There is a direct cause-and-effect relationship between the thoughts you have and the circumstances in your life. Positive self-thoughts create positive circumstances and high self-esteem. Negative self-thoughts create negative circumstances and low self-esteem.

Cause	Effect
Thoughts > Beliefs > Expectations > Attitude > Behavior > Circumstance	

Self-esteem has to do with how we think about ourselves which influences what we believe about ourselves. These beliefs shape our expectations, attitudes, and behavior to eventually create the circumstances of our life. We know that children who have low self-esteem think poorly of themselves. And if a child is thinking poorly of him- or herself surely the circumstances of his or her life will not be too positive.

Wise men and philosophers throughout the ages have disagreed on many things, but many are in unanimous agreement on one point: we become what we think about! Ralph Waldo Emerson, the great poet, philosopher and essayist, once said, "We become what we think about, all day long." Marcus Aurelius, the powerful Roman emperor, put it this way, "A man's life is what his thoughts make of it." And in the Bible we find, "For as a man thinketh in his heart, so is he."

Psychologists call it "self-talk" or "internal dialogue." Children and sometimes adults, for that matter, are not always aware of the thoughts they have about themselves. And unfortunately sometimes those thoughts can be negative or self-defeating.

Becoming aware of the fact that we all engage in self-talk is an important step towards enhancing self-esteem. With the knowledge that we do in fact talk to ourselves, we can become aware of the negative little "messages" that we hurt ourselves with throughout the day. When we become aware of these self-limiting thoughts we can then make a conscious effort to change those negative self-thoughts into positive affirming thoughts. We can help our students do this through the process of creating affirming declarations. Remember, we feel the way we think. And in order to change the way we feel we can start by changing the way we think. It's time for our students to start thinking well of themselves!

GA1501

Affirming Declarations

We learn to habitually think well of ourselves through the use of affirmations. Affirmations are positive statements declaring a desired objective as if it were already true. Affirmations are used to overcome negative self-talk, attitudes, and beliefs.

When we repeatedly read, write, or recite a positive statement, eventually over time that statement becomes something that we begin to feel comfortable with. The new thought becomes something that we begin to believe. For example, let's say that a student has a fear of speaking in front of a large audience. Many different negative things come to mind when given the task of having to present to a group. That student may envision messing up the whole presentation, slurring words, dropping notes, or forgetting what to say. All of this is just a negative image that has been created in the mind. With the use of a positive statement combined with the mental rehearsal corresponding to that positive statement, a student can create a more positive outcome. Perhaps that student could use an affirming declaration such as, "I am comfortably and calmly speaking in front of any number of people." Let's learn exactly how to write effective affirming declarations.

Writing Effective Affirming Declarations:

1. Start with the words *I am . . . I can . . . My . . .* Be personal.

2. Write the affirming declaration in the present tense. The statement should be written as if you have already acquired the desired objective.
   > Example: "I am an A student."
   > Not: "I am receiving an A grade in school."

3. Phrase affirming declarations in the positive. Affirm what you want, not what you don't want.
   > Example: "I am confidently speaking up in class."
   > Not: "I am not afraid to speak up in class."

4. The shorter and simpler the affirming declaration, the more effective. It should convey a strong feeling.

5. Write the affirming declaration as specific to a desired objective as possible. Vague declarations produce vague results.

6. Always choose an affirming declaration that feels totally right for you.

One important point to remember is that reciting or writing affirmations should be practiced consistently over time. In order to promote and envelop a particular affirmation as part of one's self-concept, it must take the place of an old habit or belief. New habits or beliefs take time to develop.

GA1501

Affirming Declaration Examples

Self-Esteem

I love and appreciate myself just as I am.

I am a special and unique person.

I am whole and complete, perfect the way I am.

Action

I am learning more easily and quickly every day.

I express myself fully and clearly at all times.

I have all the strength and energy necessary to create whatever I desire.

Goal

I am joyfully receiving an A in math on my report card.

I am proudly holding my certificate for being on the honor roll.

GA1501

Developing Affirming Declarations

Goal: To help determine goals and identify and affirm personal attributes. Students will develop positive thinking behavior to develop greater self-esteem.

Time: Several days

Setting: Classroom

Materials: Paper, pencils, markers, crayons, index cards, poster board or construction paper, magazines, scissors, paint

Procedure:

1. **Write Goals:** Invite your students to think of three goals they would like to achieve by the end of the school year. Have the students write those goals in as concrete a form as possible. The goals should be written in sensory specific form stating quantity and time. Discuss how their goals can be accomplished and how they will feel when they have achieved their goals. This will help to create interest and enthusiasm, motivating them to action.

2. **Identify Strengths:** Students identify ten strengths they have which will help them to accomplish their goals. Make sure that the students list ten strengths. You may find that a number of the students will have difficulty coming up with ten strengths they possess.

3. **Wish List:** Students make their "wish" list. Students list everything they want. Help the students to concentrate in three specific areas which will help to develop a new self-concept. These areas are (1) who they want to be, (2) what they want to do, and (3) what they want to have. Share with the students some of your desires. In the beginning of the exercise students think this is very easy; but after they list those things that they want, some may reach roadblocks simply because they have never been asked what they really want out of life. Stretching the students to list particular attributes or qualities they wish to obtain can be a challenge.

4. **Create the Affirming Declaration:** At this time your students have three lists: goals, strengths, and wishes. From these three lists students will develop their affirmation statements. The affirming declaration will address their goals and desires. Make sure the students include their strengths as they create their affirming declarations.

5. **Index Cards:** Using index cards, have your students write their affirming declaration on one side and on the opposite side have your students draw a picture or visual image representing the declaration.

6. **Posters or Collages:** Students create posters or collages illustrating their affirming declarations. Students should write the declaration somewhere on the poster. Creating the poster or collage incorporates the visual image of the affirming declaration quite strongly. Hanging the posters and collages in the classroom encourages the students to interact with the images they wish to acquire.

7. **Oral Language:** Once the class has completed their affirming declarations have them repeat the positive statements internally or aloud. The students may say them in unison or practice their handwriting skills by writing them down. The key is constant repetition over time. Remember, Belief = Habits of Thought.

GA1501

Moving Beyond Affirming Declarations: Questions!

"Ask, and ye shall receive."

What is thinking? Thinking is the process of asking and answering questions. If we believe that we become what we think about, then what we think about is a direct result of the questions we ask—either consciously or subconsciously.

Think about it . . .

Question: Who are the best question askers in the world? Answer: Kids!
Kids ask questions all day long. "Where do I come from?" "What happens to the sun at night?" "How big is the world?" "Why do I have to do my homework?"

Why do they do it? Because children are constantly making evaluations about what things mean and what decisions to make. They are starting to develop beliefs that will shape their lives. They're little learning machines, and the way they learn is by asking questions—questions they ask of themselves and others.

The key here is to help children ask the right questions. Quality questions create a quality life. If children are constantly asking questions like, "Why don't I ever do well in school?" "How come nobody likes me?" you can bet the answers are going to be disempowering! There's no way they could feel good about their answers! On the other hand if children ask, "What am I happy about?" or "What could I be happy about?" they will look for references to answer that question. References come in the form of personal experiences, information, and imagination. The children will start thinking back to what they have personally experienced that was fun and happy; they will focus on information in the present that will give them reason to feel happy; and they can imagine future experiences that could make them happy.

If we continue to ask any question, we will eventually receive an answer. The questions that we ask will determine how we feel, our picture of who we are, and what we need to do to realize our dreams. The key is to ask the right questions consistently to help us experience more joyful, exciting, and fulfilling lives.

GA1501

Find the Answers!

1. What am I happy about? What could I be happy about?

_____

_____

2. What am I excited about? What could I be excited about?

_____

_____

3. What am I proud of? What could I be proud of?

_____

_____

4. How am I having fun? How could I be having fun?

_____

_____

5. What am I thankful for? What could I be thankful for?

_____

_____

6. Who loves me?

_____

_____

7. Whom do I love?

_____

_____

8. What have I learned today?

_____

_____

GA1501

Self-Esteem Through Movement

What do you see young children doing when they're intensively involved in play? They move! They move all over and under and around and through the place. They roll like a log or a ball; they crawl, jump, hop, skip, run, slide, twist, and fall. Then they get back up and start all over again. And what do we do when we get them in the classroom? We have them keep their hands and feet still, sit in tiny little chairs, at neat little square desks with little "blinders" around them (carrells) to keep them focused on their own little square papers. We teach them to sit still and be quiet. But do we encourage and provide opportunities for children to explore the world around them in every way they can imagine?

We now understand that movement in space, freedom to explore the environment, and developing bodily abilities are links to intellectual development. Physical movement for very young children develops math skills, problem-solving skills, and spatial-visual skills that contribute to reading readiness. Physical movement may also help to prevent degenerative diseases, improve overall physical condition, maintain emotional balance, and promote a sense of social effectiveness. Children feel healthy and energized when provided with the opportunity to move.

Movement Skills and Body Image

A child will begin to internalize a positive body image when provided with opportunities to become aware of how one's body moves and adjusts to flow, weight, time, and space. The child, when given the opportunity to explore movement, begins to appreciate and enjoy the aesthetic and expressive elements of the body. As teachers, our goal is to help children become aware of how they move and to enjoy moving their bodies. We must guide children in determining what bodily expressions are appropriate, comfortable, celebratory, or joyous. Presenting specific movement activities will help children to internalize a positive body image.

Body Language

A large sense of our self resides in our body. We must acknowledge that there is a mind-body or body-mind link that affects the way we think of ourselves. The mind-body linkage is a two-way street, whereby we receive messages from our body which influence our mind and the way we think of ourselves. For some of us this is a difficult concept to accept. Most of us will acknowledge the existence of techniques that affect the body, for example stress reduction methods such as meditation or placebo drugs that eliminate illnesses. However, the body communicates to the mind as well. Changing the mind or the way we think and feel about ourselves can begin with changing the body.

Try standing with your shoulders slumped, with your head hanging down, with a frown on your face and give a big "Woe is me" sigh. How does that feel? Pretty depressing, right? Now try standing tall and confident and proud. Pull your shoulders back, put a smile on your face, breathe deeply and exhale quickly, and see what happens to the way you think and feel about yourself. I dare you to tell me that you don't start feeling more confident and happy. When we adapt the physiology of a confident person, we develop the attitude of a confident person. The idea here is to provide opportunities for our students to create patterns of movement that help them feel confident, strong, beautiful, flexible, powerful, and fun!

GA1501

Here are four ideas to get you started!

Five Smiles a Day: At five different times during the day, just shout out, "It's smile time!" Everybody looks around the room and watches everybody smiling. Before you know it everyone is laughing!

Jump for Joy! Have your class get out of their seats and jump for joy.

Gold Medalists: Everyone, while at his or her seat or while standing or walking in line, will act like a champion who just received a gold medal. Ask your class, "How would someone who just received a gold medal stand, how would he or she walk, how would his or her face look? Show me how!"

Classroom Skip: Have the whole class skip around the room or skip to the lunch line or the bathroom. Of course you'll have to model the behavior, so I'm sure everyone will have a smile on his or her face. That means YOU!

GA1501

Movement Exploration Activities

The following activities are designed to enhance student self-esteem by allowing children the freedom to explore their environment while solving challenging movement problems at the same time. In these activities students will combine their mental and physical skills to solve the challenges presented. When a child learns to achieve a physical challenge he or she receives personal satisfaction and feels competent.

In these activities students will be challenged to move in relation to a partner or an object. Students will experience a sense of adventure and discovery as they determine their own methods for best meeting the challenge. Presenting movement activities in this way will allow everyone to succeed because each child moves in a unique way.

Teacher Responsibilities

The teacher is the most important facilitator towards the students' enjoyment and successful completion of the movement challenges. Presenting the questions with enthusiasm and intermittent reinforcement is the teacher's primary task. It's also a great idea to set up agreements before beginning the activities. Suggested agreements are (1) Noise is kept to a minimum so that children can hear the challenges (whispering voices are suggested). (2) No one is allowed to touch or talk to a neighbor unless asked to do so. (3) Set up a stop or freeze signal beforehand. (4) Set up space boundaries for the students to move within.

Presenting the Challenges

It is important to create an environment of acceptance and nonjudgment. This is accomplished by presenting the challenges in the form of a question. The question should always be stated as, "How can you . . . ?" Stating a question in this way allows for the maximum student involvement with the most possible answers. The words "How can you . . . ?" imply that the teacher already knows the child can meet the challenges or perform the skill. When the teacher presents the question as, "Can you . . . ?" or "Show me how you can . . . " it implies that the teacher wants to see the movement and will measure or evaluate the child's response to the challenge. By presenting the challenge in the form of, "How can you . . . ?" it provides a sense of total freedom from evaluation and judgment.

The Movement Activities

The two activities provided, Beanbag and Me and Partners and Boxes, were designed for children in kindergarten through second grade. These two activities are presented as examples of what the self-contained elementary school teacher can do to provide movement challenges. Other objects can be substituted in place of the beanbags or cardboard boxes, such as Hula-Hoops™, balls, towels, chairs, desks, inner tubes, etc. The possibilities are endless and totally dependent upon the imagination of the teacher and children.

GA1501

Movement challenges can also be presented that will allow children to move without relation to an object. In these activities children should still be presented with the question, "How can you . . . ?" and be challenged to move in relation to:

• Shape (twisted, long, short, thin, wide, round, etc.)
• Position (bend, stoop, squat)
• Direction (backward, forward, sideways, up, down)
• Speed (slow, medium, fast)
• Level (high, medium, low)
• Weight (heavy, light)
• Accelerate, Decelerate
• Roll, Skip, Jump, Hop, Shuffle, Slide, Run, Jog, etc.

GA1501

Beanbag and Me

Goal: Students will identify their body parts as they move a beanbag in relation to their whole body and specific body parts. Students will balance a beanbag on specific body parts while moving through space.

Time: 20-30 minutes

Setting: Classroom, gymnasium, or outside

Materials: One beanbag for each student

Procedure: Have your students take off their shoes and give each one a beanbag. Then ask the following questions and have fun watching the activity.

- How can you put the beanbag on your head and balance it there without touching it with your hands? How can you put the beanbag on your shoulder and balance it there without using your hands?

- How can you put the beanbag on your arm and keep it there without using your hands? On your elbow? On your wrist? How can you put the beanbag on the back of your hand and keep it there without using your other hand?

- How can you put the beanbag on your leg and keep it there without using your hands? On your knee? How can you put the beanbag on the top of your foot and balance it there while keeping that foot off the ground and without touching it? On the bottom of your foot?

- How can you put the beanbag on your buttocks and keep it there without using your hands? How can you put the beanbag on your back and balance it there without using your hands?

- How can you put the beanbag on your ear? How can you put the beanbag on your nose while balancing it there without touching it with your hands? On your eye?

- How can you hold the beanbag between your hand and stomach? How can you hold the beanbag between your chin and your chest?

- How can you hold the beanbag between your knee and your nose? How can you hold the beanbag between both knees? Between your elbow and your foot?

- How can you hold the beanbag between your side and your arm? How can you hold the beanbag between your shoulder and ear? Between your cheek and arm?

- How can you pick up the beanbag and hold it over your whole body?

- How can you place the beanbag in front of you? In back of you? To the side of you?

- How can you move the beanbag around you?

- How can you move the beanbag under you? How can you move the beanbag far away from you? Near you?

77

- How can you put the beanbag beside your foot? Under your back? Under your head?

- How can you balance the beanbag on your head while moving forward? On your shoulder? On your elbow?

- How can you balance the beanbag on your foot while moving forward? On your knee? On your forehead?

- From the standing position, how can you sit down while balancing the beanbag on your head? On your shoulder?

- How can you hop in place while keeping the beanbag above you?

- How can you balance the beanbag on your head while moving sideways? While moving backwards?

Partners and Boxes

Goal: Students will work cooperatively with a partner to balance, locate specific body parts, and move their bodies in relation to a cardboard box.

Time: 20-30 minutes

Setting: Classroom, gymnasium, or playground

Materials: One medium-sized cardboard box for every two students

Procedure: Have the students take off their shoes and give each pair of children one medium-sized cardboard box. Asking these questions will promote lots of fun!

- How can both of you place your arms in the box? How about your feet? Now what about your toes from only one foot each?

- How can both of you put your head in the box? Now your elbows? How about your hands only?

- How can both of you put just your chin in the box? Now one knee?

Explain to your students that now they will be working with their partners in a way where they will be touching each other in some way in order to balance together.

- How can you balance with your partner so you have only three total body parts touching the floor? (Remember, between the two students only three body parts are touching the floor.)

- How can you balance with your partner so that five body parts are touching the ground? How about seven body parts?

- How can you balance with your partner so that only two body parts are touching the ground?

- How can you balance with your partner so that five body parts are touching the ground, only this time you can't put your hands on the floor?

- How can you balance with your partner so that you have a total of eight body parts touching the ground, only this time no hands or feet?

Now back to the boxes.

- How can you work together so that the box is above both of you?

- How can you work together so that the box is behind both of you? How about beside both of you? Now between both of you?

- How can you work together to move the box around and around and around both of you?

- How can you work and move together so that the box is between your backs? How about between your chests? Now between your thighs?

GA1501

- How can you move the box so that it is under your feet? How about under your legs? Now under your arms?

- How can you move the box so that one partner's hands are inside it and the other partner's hands are under it?

- How can you move the box so that one partner's feet are inside of the box and the other partner's feet are outside the box?

- How can you move the box so that one partner's chest is under the box and the other partner's chest is over the box?

- How can you move the box so that one partner's legs are over the box and the other partner's legs are around the box?

- How can you move the box so that both of your heads are under the box?

- How can you both walk sideways with the box between you? How can you do it with no hands?

- How can you both move backwards with the box behind only one of you? How can you do it with no hands?

- How can you both stand inside the box?

- How can you both move the box back and forth between you, using only your feet to move it? Using only your heads?

- How can you both move the box back and forth between you without letting it touch the floor?

- How can you both pick up the box using only your heads? Using only your feet? Using only your elbows?

- How can one partner slide the box around the other partner?

Mastery of basic skills such as these throughout a child's life will contribute greatly to a positive self-image. Children will feel physically competent and will develop a positive attitude about their bodies; they will be in touch with their bodies; they will learn to listen to their bodies; they will look good and feel good. If teachers are really serious about enhancing their students' self-esteem, they will provide a sequential, developmental program of movement activities designed to help a child acquire a lifetime appreciation of physical movement and activity. With this, children will come to learn that they are beautiful.

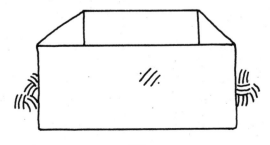

GA1501

Journal Writing for Developing Self-Awareness

In order for students to become more aware of who they are, time is needed for private self-reflection. The sentence stems provided help children to get in touch with their thoughts, feelings, and imaginations. You may find that your students have never thought about these before.

- The things I do best are . . .
- My favorite toy is . . .
- I feel very happy when . . .
- I get impatient when . . .
- I get worried when . . .
- I cry when . . .
- I try very hard to . . .
- If I had one million dollars, I would . . .
- My favorite food is . . .
- I feel nervous when . . .
- If I were a famous person, I would be . . .
- I don't like to . . .
- If I were a mouse, I would . . .
- When I'm at home my favorite thing to do is . . .
- I pout when . . .
- I like the way my . . .
- My favorite book is . . .
- I wish I could change the way other people . . .
- My favorite holiday is _____ because . . .
- When I'm in my bedroom . . .

- I feel important when . . .
- My favorite subject in school is . . .
- If I were President, I would . . .
- It embarrasses me when . . .
- I am proud of myself when . . .
- When I am very friendly, I . . .
- My body is . . .
- If I were a dog, I would . . .
- I like to play . . .
- I feel disappointed when . . .
- The things I like best about me are . . .
- Something I'd like to change is . . .
- When I go outside to play, I like to . . .
- If I were granted three wishes, I would . . .
- I feel very smart when . . .
- My favorite television show is . . .
- My favorite colors are . . .
- One thing I'd like to change about myself is . . .
- When I'm at home with my family, I like to . . .
- If I could go anywhere in the whole world, I would . . .

GA1501

Interdisciplinary Activities

Multicultural Education

Goal: Students will demonstrate knowledge of and respect for cultural traditions of Japan.
Time: Several days
Setting: Classroom
Materials: One large piece of construction paper, newspaper, pipe cleaner, paint or markers, crepe paper, glue, scissors, pencil
Procedure: Using various resources from your school library, have your students research the special celebration known as Children's Day held on May 5 in Japan. Originally this festival was known as Boy's Day, but after World War II the Japanese decided to honor all of its children. What your students will find is that on this day special fish made of paper or cloth are flown on bamboo poles in front of most homes. Known to the Japanese as *koinobori,* the paper fish are models of a kind of carp that had to battle their way upstream against strong currents. In times past the Japanese wanted boys to become strong warriors, and it was thought that these fish would be a good symbol for boys. Today, as this festival is observed, it is hoped that all young boys and girls will also grow to be brave and powerful like the carp fish. After your students finish with their research invite them to make their own carp kite following the directions below.

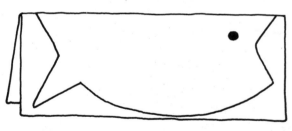

Fold a large piece of construction paper in half the long way. Draw the outline of a carp on one half of the paper using the fold as the center. Then cut out the fish.

Open up the carp fish and decorate it with crepe paper, color it, paint it, etc.

Tape a pipe cleaner inside the edge of the carp's mouth to reinforce it. Then fold the paper around the pipe cleaner to hide it.

Finally, glue the edges of your carp fish while leaving a large opening for the mouth. Stuff it with newspapers and then if you have a windy day, take the carp kite outside, attach it to a pole and watch it fly.

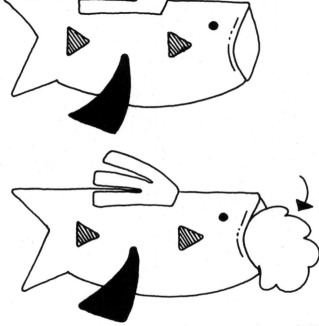

Art

Origami

Goal: Students will gain an appreciation of Japanese artistic heritage.
Time: Several days
Setting: Classroom
Materials: Several square pieces of paper with one side colored for each student
Procedure: The Japanese have developed many paper-folding art projects that your students can construct and play with: boats, butterflies, pigs, turtles, and even crows! Your school library should have at least one book on the subject. Try to find *The ABC's of Origami* by Claude Sarasas (Charles E. Tuttle Company, Inc., 1989) for twenty-six great ideas. All of the origami projects are constructed from folded squares of paper and in most cases only one square is needed. In some cases several folded squares have to be fixed together and for these you'll need a little glue. Try to find paper with one colored side for an authentic look. For an additional literature activity, read *Sadako and the Thousand Paper Cranes* by Eleanor Coerr (Dell) to your students as they construct their origami sculptures.

Language Arts

My Family and Me!

Goal: Students will understand that their cultural background is an important part of their identity.
Time: Several days
Setting: Classroom
Materials: Work sheets, book-making materials
Procedure: Begin this activity by sharing with your students your family's past. Maybe you'll want to bring a family photo album to show, explain where your family came from, talk about the special holidays and ethnic dishes that your family enjoys, and of course let them know about your family's heritage and special qualities. You'll find your students extremely interested in finding out all about you! Then tell them that you'd like to know more about all of them and their families. Assign the following My Family and Me work sheet for homework. Of course you'll need to explain how to complete the assignment. When your students return to school with the completed work (hopefully the next day), talk about what they discovered. After the discussion invite your students to construct a book entitled "My Family and Me." The book can consist of two chapters, the first chapter titled "Me" and the second chapter, "My Family." The work sheet will help to organize chapter contents. Ask your students to bring photographs from home to include in the book: baby pictures, holiday pictures, pictures of family members, etc. Student-drawn illustrations will also be appropriate if photos are not available. When the books are completed, invite children to read their stories to the class.

GA1501

My Family and Me!

Name: _____ _____ _____
　　　　　　first　　　　　　　　　　middle　　　　　　　　　　last

Date of Birth: _____ _____ _____
　　　　　　　　month　　　　　　　　　　day　　　　　　　　　　year

Place of Birth: _____ _____ _____
　　　　　　　　city　　　　　　　　　　state　　　　　　　　　　country

Ask your family to help you with these questions about YOU.

When did you first begin to walk?_____

What was the first word you spoke? _____

What was your favorite toy when you were a baby?_____

What was one special thing that you did when you were:

1 year old _____

2 years old _____

3 years old _____

4 years old _____

5 years old _____

6 years old _____

7 years old _____

8 years old _____

Ask your parents to help you with these questions about YOUR FAMILY.

Father's Name _____

Mother's Name _____

Brothers' Names _____

Sisters' Names _____

What are your grandparents' names? _____

_____

From what country did your family first come? _____

When did your family first come to this country? _____

What are the languages that your family speaks, reads, or writes? ___

_____

What special holiday(s) does your family celebrate? _____

_____

What is your family's favorite food to eat? _____

What are some of the things that make your family so special? _____

_____

_____

We Speak Japanese.

We love spaghetti!

GA1501

Diamante Poem

In *Crow Boy* Chibi changes from a "forlorn little tagalong" to Crow Boy–a proud young man. With the help of his sixth grade teacher we learn of Chibi's talents and abilities. We come to like this little boy until he is no longer Chibi. He becomes Crow Boy. Write about the changes Chibi goes through in this Japanese diamante poem. Start with his nickname, "Chibi," and finish the poem with his new name, "Crow Boy."

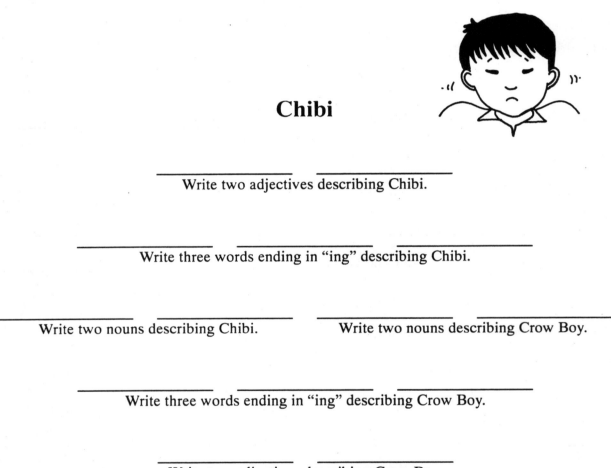

Chibi

_____ _____

Write two adjectives describing Chibi.

_____ _____ _____

Write three words ending in "ing" describing Chibi.

_____ _____   _____ _____

Write two nouns describing Chibi.   Write two nouns describing Crow Boy.

_____ _____ _____

Write three words ending in "ing" describing Crow Boy.

_____ _____

Write two adjectives describing Crow Boy.

Crow Boy

GA1501

Your Feelings

We learn in *Crow Boy* that little Chibi has many different feelings. What about you; do you have feelings? When do you have these feelings? What do you do when you have these different feelings?

I get lonely when _____

When I'm lonely I _____

I'm sad when _____

When I'm sad I _____

I'm afraid when _____

When I'm afraid I _____

I'm nervous when _____

When I'm nervous I _____

I'm happy when _____

When I'm happy I _____

I'm excited when _____

When I'm excited I _____

GA1501

Feeling Faces

Everyone has feelings, and there are many kinds of feelings. Draw a face that matches the feeling.

Draw a happy face.

Draw an angry face.

Draw a sad face.

Draw a surprised face.

Draw a confused face.

Draw a shy face.

Draw a proud face.

Draw an excited face.

Draw a frustrated face.

GA1501

Thank You, Mr. Isobe

Mr. Isobe was Chibi's sixth grade teacher. He was a very kind and friendly man. What sort of things did Chibi learn from Mr. Isobe? How did Chibi learn to be confident with Mr. Isobe's help? Pretend you are Chibi. You have just graduated from school and now you want to write him a thank-you letter. What nice things will you write to Mr. Isobe?

_____
(today's date)

_____
(your street address)

Dear Mr. Isobe,

_____

_____

_____

_____

_____

_____

_____
(closing)

_____
(your signature)

GA1501

Special Talents

In *Crow Boy* we learn of Chibi's special talents. Can you remember what his special talents were? Write down four of Chibi's special talents.

1. _____

2. _____

3. _____

4. _____

Do you have any special talents? Does your teacher know of your special talents? Write down two special talents that you have.

1. _____

2. _____

Draw a picture of you using one of your special talents. The class, your teacher, and the world are waiting to know what your special talent is!

GA1501

What Kind of Person Are You?

I'm a person who . . .

likes _____

dislikes _____

can _____

would never _____

loves to _____

wants to learn how to _____

used to be afraid of _____

is really good at _____

is really happy about _____

gets really angry when _____

has the good habit of _____

has the bad habit of _____

wishes I could change the way other people _____

would like to change the way I _____

will someday _____

   GA1501

In the puzzle below write in each of the ten pieces one word that will answer the question "Who am I?" Write down your answers quickly, taking the first words that pop into your head. Try to think of words that are nouns (student, boy, singer) and adjectives (friendly, funny, shy) to complete the puzzle. When you are finished cut out the pieces, put the puzzle together, and glue it on a sheet of construction paper. Then take a look at your words. Each of the words that you have written is like a piece of a puzzle that is YOU! You can learn to like yourself for what you are: an individual, special in your own unique way.

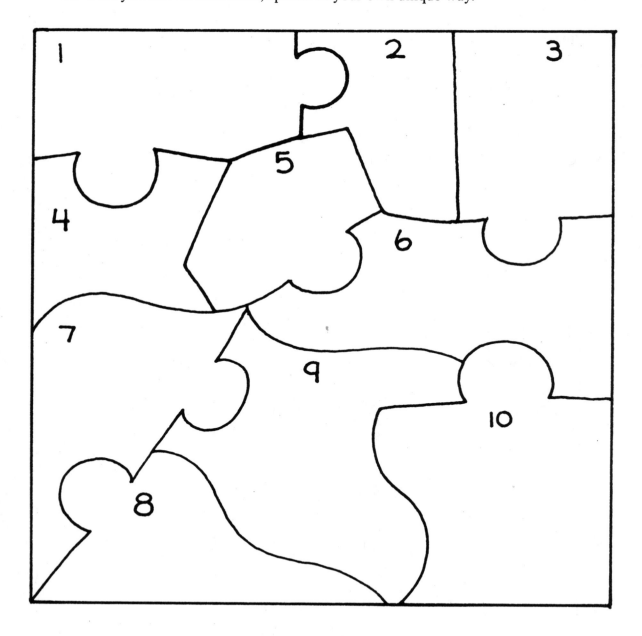

My Opposite and Me

Think of eight words that describe you and write them in the circles on the ME side. Then on the OPPOSITE side, write the opposite or the antonym to each word you wrote on the ME side. Now, look at the OPPOSITE side. Do any of those words describe the way you are sometimes? Maybe they do. Sometimes it's important to know that we behave many different ways. If you think you are shy, mean or cowardly, you may discover that sometimes you are outgoing, kind, and courageous. Finally, write an *X* on the line joining the two sides to show where your behavior falls most often between the words you used to describe yourself and your opposites. Becoming aware of who you are means understanding all of the behaviors that make you YOU.

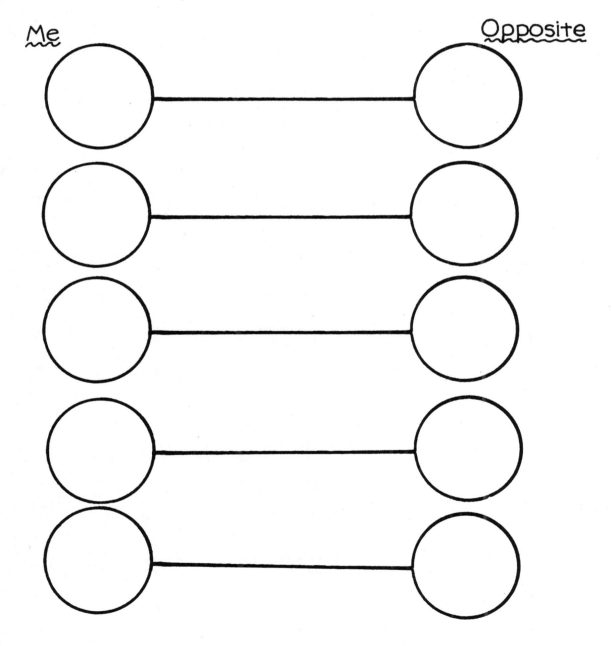

Me

Opposite

GA1501

There's No One Like Me

by Mark Ledwig

We all have certain songs that help to make us feel good. Here's a song that does just that. When you sing this song, with your teacher's help, you'll feel good about the most important person in the world–YOU!

I'm not real-ly brag-gin', 'cause it's clear-ly plain to see (you'll see) I'm a spec-ial per-son, I know there's no one like me. (no one) I won't say I'm per-fect but I'm aw-fully good in-deed. There's no one, there's no one like me.

94

GA1501

95

GA1501

Self-Awareness Certificate

This certificate is awarded to _____ for being a very special and unique person. In discovering your outstanding qualities and characteristics you have also taught others in our classroom how to be proud of who we are.

This certificate will help to show others that in the whole wide world there is no one else like _____!

Congratulations,

_____!

Awarded on the _____ day of _____

Signed: _____
(teacher)

Determining a Purpose

"Strange is our situation here upon earth. Each of us comes for a short visit, not knowing why, but sometimes seeming to divine a purpose."
— Albert Einstein

Build a Mission with Responsibility

This is perhaps the most powerful step in the process of developing self-esteem. How many people do you know that have determined exactly what they want for their lives? Do they plan a course by which to acquire their desires and virtues? Do they measure their progress towards their goals? Do they even have any goals? Students who have a clear sense of purpose, who set worthwhile goals for themselves, and then take the actions and risks essential to achieve them are destined to be more intrinsically motivated in your classroom—and in life. When we provide opportunities for students to set goals, devise plans for attainment, and then watch them actually reach the goals, we have helped to create a positive experience for children that may have no equal. We have helped to motivate, to empower, and to liberate those children.

Determining a Purpose with *The Little Engine That Could*

In this story, after a happy little train carrying wonderful little toys for the children on the other side of the mountain breaks down, the toys are faced with a dilemma. They have to make it to the other side. They ask a couple of "stuck-up" trains to take them over, but they're too important to bother with a silly bunch of toys. They ask a rusty old engine, but this engine can't work up the strength anymore to do the job. He's old and tired. Then a Little Blue Engine comes chugging merrily along and the toys ask her. But she's never been over the mountain before! But the toys have to make it to the children on the other side. Will she, or won't she? Can she, or can't she? The Little Blue Engine has to make a decision. She decides; she sets a goal; she determines her purpose! She thinks she can, she thinks she can, she thinks she can, and SHE DOES! She makes it over the mountain and the funny little clown and all the dolls and all the toys are happy.

"'Hurray, hurray,' cried the funny little clown and all the dolls and toys. 'The good little boys and girls in the city will be happy because you helped us, kind Little Blue Engine.'

"And the Little Blue Engine smiled and seemed to say as she puffed steadily down the mountain . . . 'I thought I could. I thought I could. I thought I could. I thought I could. I thought I could. I thought I could.'" [1]

---
1. From THE LITTLE ENGINE THAT COULD retold by Watty Piper. Copyright 1930, © 1958 by Platt & Munk, Co. THE LITTLE ENGINE THAT COULD is a trademark of Platt & Munk, Co. and is used by permission.

Every time I read this story I want to get up out of my chair and do something really important. I get so excited! And because I'm into the story, or more specifically the theme of the story, most everyone I read this story to wants to get up out of his or her chair and do something really important too. That's the way kids need to feel. They also need to think that no matter what it is they choose to do, that if they set their minds to it, there is nothing they can't do. If you don't believe this, then you've just determined your own self-imposed limitation. And when you project these limitations onto children, you're facilitating the sense of helplessness that goes along with low self-esteem. I truly believe that kids can do anything they want to do. Hey, I'm not saying it's going to be easy, but if they're willing to work at it, really work at it, their dreams can come true.

Thematic Unit:	Purpose
Core Literature:	*The Little Engine That Could* by Watty Piper (Platt & Munk, Co.)
Extended Literature:	*Swimmy* by Leo Lionni (Pantheon)
	Jack and the Beanstalk by Steven Kellogg (Morrow Junior Books)
Recreational Literature:	Books on trains, railroad, and transportation

Additional Literature Supporting the Theme of Purpose

Altogether, One at a Time by E.L. Konigsburg (Atheneum)
. . . And Now Miguel by Joseph Krumgold (Crowell)
And Then What Happened, Paul Revere? by Jean Fritz (Coward)
Anpao: An American Indian Odyssey by Jamake Highwater
The Blanket That Had to Go by Nancy Evans (Putnam)
Bread and Jam for Francis by Russell Hoban (Harper & Row)
Bridge to Terabithia by Katherine Paterson (Avon)
Call It Courage by Armstrong Sperry (Macmillan)
Castle in the Attic by Elizabeth Winthrop (Bantam-Skylark)
The Cat Ate My Gymsuit by Paula Danzinger (Delacorta)
Courage of Sarah Noble by Alice Dalgliesh (Scribner)
Dear Mr. Henshaw by Beverly Cleary (Dell)
Every Living Thing by Cynthia Rylant (Aladdin)
Freedom Train: The Story of Harriet Tubman by Dorothy Sterling (Doubleday & Co.)
The Gift of the Sacred Dog by Paul Goble (Bradbury Press)
Glorious Flight by Alice and Martin Provenson (Viking Press)
Harriet the Spy by Louise Fitzhugh (Harper & Row)
Hatchet by Gary Paulsen (Bradbury Press)
Little Bear by Else Minarik (Harper & Row)
Number the Stars by Lois Lowry (Houghton Mifflin)
The Red Badge of Courage by Stephen Crane (Bantam Books)
Sir Gawain and the Loathly Lady by Selina Hastings (Lothrop, Lee & Shepard Books)
The Wizard of Oz by Frank Baum (Bobley Publications)
Wonderful Flight to Mushroom Planet by Eleanor Cameron (Little)

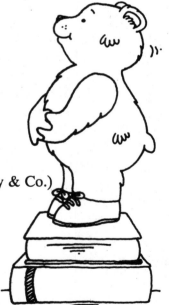

GA1501

Supporting Subthemes of Purpose

The following subthemes help to support or complement this fourth step of enhancing self-esteem—determining a purpose. Subthemes provide a tangent for either the teacher or the students to take when developing understanding of the theme of purpose.

- Adventure
- Love
- Education
- Environment
- Imagination
- Work
- Design
- Ambition

- Quest
- Duty
- Pleasure
- Revolution
- Survival
- Career
- Free Will
- Plan

- Goals
- Solving Problems
- Making Decisions
- Motivation
- Explorers
- Action
- Search

Self-Esteem Theme Objectives

The teacher will . . .

1. **Teach the skills of setting effective goals.** Goals serve as the stimulus for life, they keep us moving forward, and they provide direction for our future. Each time students reach goals they become motivated in the process. They begin to see themselves as capable and as achievers.

2. **Teach children how to record their performance.** Teach students to record the successful achievement of assignments on a chart. This will provide an opportunity for the children to regularly view their progress towards personal goals. Children need to see that they are constantly growing and progressing; sometimes a quarterly report card is not enough. This will motivate them to continue working hard to accumulate more points, stars, or smiling faces.

3. **Teach decision making and problem-solving skills.** When children learn to solve their own problems, they develop personal responsibility and accountability. As children become more responsible, they realize that they have more power and control over their lives. They stop blaming others and begin realizing that they do, in fact, create their own reality.

The students will . . .

- Develop a feeling of purpose and motivation in life.
- Become willing to take responsibility for the consequences of decisions.
- Develop more self-confidence.
- Learn that life has meaning.

99

GA1501

Goal-Setting Activities

Everybody dreams of becoming somebody important. No matter who we are or where we come from, deep down inside, all of us believe that we're special. Just ask any child and he or she will tell you. Children all dream of becoming something special: astronauts, teachers, doctors, lawyers, or baseball players.

I remember this story about a special little boy who lived in the run-down section of San Francisco. This was a little boy who had permanently bowed legs as a result of a malnutrition condition called rickets. His legs were so skinny that his friends called him "Pencil Legs." This little boy wanted more than anything to become a professional football player–he wanted to be a famous running back. To this little boy, his favorite team, the Cleveland Browns, was more than just an ordinary football team because the great running back Jim Brown was on their roster.

One day the Cleveland Browns were in the boy's home city of San Francisco to play against the 49ers. So the little boy went to the stadium to watch the game. But when he got there he soon discovered that he didn't have enough money to get in to see the game. He decided to wait outside the stadium in hopes of catching a glimpse of his great idol, Jim Brown, when he came out of the locker room after the game. So he waited and waited and when the game was over, suddenly from around the corner the great Jim Brown appeared. The little boy stood there looking up in total awe. His eyes opened wide and his mouth dropped open. Nervously he blurted out, "Mr. Brown, Mr. Brown, you're my hero, Mr. Brown!" "Sure, kid," Brown said as he continued walking. But the little boy was persistent so he followed behind and said, "But Mr. Brown, I watch you on television every chance I get, I collect all your pictures, and I know every one of your records!" "Great, kid. Keep me in your dreams," Brown said, somewhat irritated by the little boy's persistence. Finally the little boy ran up alongside Jim Brown, tugged on his shirt, and said, "Mr. Brown, not only do I know all of your records, but I plan to break every one of them!" With that statement Jim Brown stopped dead in his tracks, he turned around, knelt down and asked, "What's your name, kid?" The little kid smiled because he knew he had his attention now, and said, "My name's Simpson, sir. My friends just call me O.J."

Great accomplishments, fulfilled dreams, and broken records all start with a burning desire to make them happen. There was no doubt in that young O.J. Simpson's mind that his name would go down in the record books. And the rest, as they say, is history. That little O.J. did go on to break every one of Jim Brown's records. That little boy had a goal, a goal that to many would have seemed impossible to achieve. But setting goals can provide the inspiration and focus to turn the invisible into the visible. As teachers we have a responsibility to inspire our students. One way to do this is to help our students set goals. Students need to be around teachers who inspire and encourage them to be all that they can be. Mark Twain once said, "Stay away from people who try to belittle your ambitions, small people always do that, but the really great make you feel that you too can be great." Teachers must help their students find a dream and achieve it.

"The mediocre teacher tells, the good teacher explains, the super teacher shows, THE GREAT ONE INSPIRES."

Effective Goal Setting

One of the best ways to help a student feel competent and capable is through the positive experience of achieving a personal goal. Goal setting is a useful and applicable esteem enhancer; however, it is far from common educational practice. Research tells us that 87 percent of us have no specific goals or plans for our lives. We're blindly pursuing life with no vision of where we're headed. Of the remaining 13 percent who do have goals, only 3 percent actually write their goals down. It is that 3 percent who will actually accomplish 50 to 100 times more throughout the course of their lifetimes, simply because they write their goals down.

Effective goals must be:

1. **Conceivable:** Students must be able to picture or visualize exactly what it is they want to accomplish.

2. **Measurable:** All goals must state quantity and time specifically. Goals are dreams with a deadline.

3. **Achievable:** Goals should be based on a student's current strengths and abilities.

4. **Sequential:** Teachers can help students set short, intermediate, and long-term goals.

5. **Believable:** A student's goals must be within his or her current value system.

6. **Written down, stated with no alternative.**

Sample Goals:

I will receive a B on my spelling quiz on Friday, October 23, 1994.

I will perform 45 sit-ups within 60 seconds on Wednesday, March 15, 1995.

I will be on the Honor Roll the second grading period of this year.

I will be a first-string quarterback on the school football team by September.

GA1501

Goal-Setting Steps

Now that we know exactly what is necessary to write effective goals, it's time to go through the process of determining what goals to write. You don't want to just start writing any old goal; that would be too rash. Let's follow these steps toward writing successful goals.

1. **Determine where you are now.** Define exactly where you or the student is in the particular area of focus. Example: In math Johnny is receiving a C.

2. **Identify your dreams and desires.** Determine exactly where you want to go. If you were guaranteed 100 percent success in whatever you attempted, what would you go for? Maybe eventually Johnny wants to be a straight A student. He definitely wants an A in math.

3. **State why you would like to achieve these goals.** The reasons why you want to achieve any worthy goal are going to provide you with the motivation to relentlessly pursue the desire. Maybe Johnny will say he will get a huge reward from his parents at home, or he will be proud of himself.

4. **Write down the goal.** Specifically state quantity and time. Example: Johnny writes the goal, I will receive an A+ on my math quiz on Friday, March 7.

5. **Identify your resources.** What help will you need to achieve your goal? What books will you need to study? Who can I ask for help? Johnny writes: his older sister, his dad who is a whiz at math, his book, and his friend Sam.

6. **Establish a plan.** Work backwards from your ultimate goal and determine what you can do today to help support your goal. Example: Johnny writes that in order to be a straight A student he must ace all his tests, ace his quizzes, do some extra credit work, and do his homework today.

7. **Take action.** Do something today, NOW! Johnny gets started working hard in math today in class.

8. **Acknowledge yourself.** If you accomplished your goal, CELEBRATE! YOU DESERVE IT! Johnny gets his reward from home and goes out and buys himself a huge banana split from the corner ice cream parlor. If you missed your goal, go back and evaluate what you could have done differently. Remember, change your actions and your results will change.

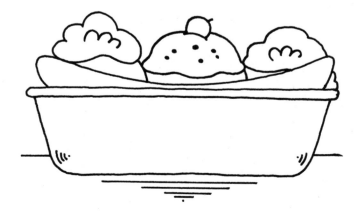

Get Your Goal

If you are going to get a goal, you must have a plan. Let's start right now with a way to get your goal!

Describe what your grade or situation is like right now.
(Example: Right now I'm getting a C in math and also a C in science.)

_____

_____

_____

Describe what your goal will look, feel, and sound like.
(Example: I will be getting an A in math and science; my teacher will say, "Good job." I will feel proud.)

_____

_____

_____

List the reasons WHY you would like to accomplish your goal.
(Example: Because I will be rewarded at home, my parents will tell me how proud they are, and I'll feel good about myself.)

_____

_____

_____

Write your goals.

I will _____

by _____

I will _____

by _____

I will _____

by _____

Write the ways you will use to reach your goals.
(Example: I will ask my teacher for extra help; I will ask my older brother to tutor me; I will go to the library to study.)

_____

_____

_____

DEVELOP YOUR PLAN: Start with your goal and work backwards until you can find something that you can do TODAY to support your goals.
(Example: I will get an A on my last test before my report card comes out; I will get an A on my quizzes; I will get an A on my homework assignments; I will study hard tonight.)

5. _____

4. _____

3. _____

2. _____

1. _____

Now . . . Get Started; Take ACTION!

GA1501

Weekly Goals

Example:
Math
I will receive an A+ on my math
quiz on Friday, April 21, 1995.

_____ _____

Subject	Written Goal	I Missed My Goal	I Made My Goal
1. _____	_____	_____	_____
	_____		
2. _____	_____	_____	_____
	_____		
3. _____	_____	_____	_____
	_____		
4. _____	_____	_____	_____
	_____		
5. _____	_____	_____	_____
	_____		
6. _____	_____	_____	_____

GA1501

Fitness Goals

Your Name:_____

What are your scores now?

Sit-Ups:_____   Pull-Ups:_____

Sit and Reach:_____   Shuttle Run: _____

Mile Run: _____

Goals:

I will complete _____ sit-ups in 60 seconds by _____.
                                                            (date)

I will complete _____ pull-ups by _____.
                                                   (date)

I will stretch to _____ in the sit-and-reach test by _____.
                                                                 (date)

I will complete the shuttle run test in _____ seconds by _____.
                                                                      (date)

I will complete the mile run in _____ minutes by _____.
                                                             (date)

Hurray for Fitness!

GA1501

Interviews

Do you know what you will be doing after elementary school? What about your friends? Do they know? Will you be going to school? Will you be in a special club or on a sports team? What about when you grow up and become an adult? What will you do then? Will you be working and making money? Will you have a family? Answer the questions for yourself first and then interview a few friends.

Your Name:_____ Age: _____

Boy or Girl:_____

What do you think you will do after elementary school?

_____

_____

What do you think you will be doing when you're 13?

_____

_____

Your Friend's Name:_____ Age: _____

Boy or Girl:_____

What do you think you will do after elementary school?

_____

_____

What do you think you will be doing when you're 13?

_____

_____

GA1501

Your Friend's Name:_____ Age: _____

Boy or Girl:_____

What do you think you will do after elementary school?

_____

_____

What do you think you will be doing when you're 13?

_____

_____

Your Friend's Name:_____ Age: _____

Boy or Girl:_____

What do you think you will do after elementary school?

_____

_____

What do you think you will be doing when you're 13?

_____

_____

Your Friend's Name:_____ Age: _____

Boy or Girl:_____

What do you think you will do after elementary school?

_____

_____

What do you think you will be doing when you're 13?

_____

_____

My Treasure Map

Goal: Students will develop a list of primary goals, select one goal, and create a collage (visual image) of that goal. The treasure map is used to facilitate the manifestation of a specific goal.

Time: Several days

Setting: Classroom

Materials: Magazines, glue, scissors, markers, construction paper, list of cut-and-paste affirmations, photograph of each student

Procedure:

Begin the lesson by stating that all successful people have had things they wished to accomplish in their lifetime. These "things" could be anything from going to Disneyland, attending college, buying a new car, starting a family, or becoming a doctor. We call these "things" goals. Explain that goals are an achievement toward which effort is directed, something we want to accomplish which we are willing to work for. Everyone wants something for his or her life. Everyone wants to be or do something important.

Share some of the things you (the teacher) have as goals. Then ask the class, "Who has a goal that he or she is willing to work for?" "What kinds of achievements do you desire?"

Write your goal. Now that the teacher has explained what goals are and the class has discussed some of their goals, have the students write on a piece of paper five goals that they have. After the students have written down their goals explain that they are to select one goal that they have high hopes of achieving. Have the students write these goals as affirmations, claiming the desired goals as if they have already been achieved. Example: "I am enjoying myself as a member of the debate team at _____ School." This is the goal that will be used on the treasure map.

Include a photograph. Assign for homework the task of bringing to school one recent photograph to include on the treasure map. (The teacher may need to provide a Polaroid™ photo of each student who is unable to find a recent photo.) A photo displayed on the treasure map will visually connect the child to the desired goal. Try to have the photo portraying the child doing, having, or being the desired goal.

The Next Day: Students begin the process of cutting out pictures from magazines and the "Cut-and-Paste Affirming Declaration and Words" from the work sheet provided that depict and reflect their goals as if they have already occurred. The pictures and words used on the collage should represent what they would experience with the achievement of their goals. Make sure to have each student include affirming declarations that support the desired goal on the collage.

Color: Use different colors on your treasure map. Color intensifies the energy of the image. Different colors represent different areas of our life: blue, intellectual achievement; green, career and money; white, spiritual; yellow and orange, health and energy; pink and red, relationships and romance. Perhaps you can provide different colored pieces of construction paper and let the students choose whatever colors they desire.

Plan and paste. Once each student has the written goal, pictures, words, affirming declarations and photograph gathered, he or she can arrange them on paper of various sizes. Colored construction paper works nicely. Once students are satisfied with their arrangements, hand out the glue and paste away! They have just created their treasure maps.

A treasure map is a visual image used to stimulate creativity to create a desired goal. It affirms the goal as already achieved, thereby acting as a "blueprint" to support the realization of a worthy desire. Treasure mapping provides a systematic approach toward manifesting a personal treasure!

Extension Activity: Treasure maps represent a very private part of a student. Depending on the level of trust and intimacy of the classroom, students can share their treasure maps with those who will provide support and nurturance. Perhaps, if willing, students can place their maps on bulletin boards, where they can be viewed throughout the day. If the level of trust and intimacy is low in the classroom, or if students feel uncomfortable displaying their treasure maps, allow them to take their maps home to be put in a private place to be viewed only by them. Spending a few quiet moments each day viewing the treasure map will intensify the creative process of discovering methods to achieve the goal.

Extension Activity: Have the children write responses to the following questions in their journals.

    What are you doing at this time to support your goals?

    How do you feel now that you have a clear picture of your goal?

    What is it like now that you have achieved your goal? (Pretending)

Cut-and-Paste Affirming Declarations and Words

PERFECT: I am perfect the way I am.

IMPORTANT: I am the most important, interesting person in my life.
            I am a vital person.

SMART: I am an intelligent person.
            I have within myself the answer to all my needs.

POWER: I am a powerful person.

ACCEPTANCE: I accept myself just the way I am.

UNIQUE: I am unique; there's no one like me.
            I am free to be me.

HAPPINESS: My life is filled with joy and happiness.
            I choose to be happy.
            I am responsible for my own happiness.

BEAUTY: I am a beautiful person, full of life and energy.

RESPONSIBLE: I am responsible for all my actions and decisions.
            I can ask for what I want.

CONFIDENCE: I exude self-confidence and self-respect.
            I trust myself, my feelings, and my thinking. I decide!

PLAY: I have the right to be fun and playful.
            I am a playful person.

GA1501

POTENTIAL: I have unlimited potential.
            I can accomplish anything.

COURAGE: I am courageous and undismayed in the face of odds.
            I am a very brave person.

LOVE: I am happily loving myself just the way I am.
            I am enjoying loving myself and others.
            I am lovable, capable, and significant.

SMART: I am scoring well on all my tests.
            I am finding it easier and easier to do all my homework.

STRENGTH: I have a strong mind and body.

HEALTH: I am in great shape. I take care of my body with plenty of
            exercise and good foods.

Solving Relationship Problems

Low self-esteem has a profound negative effect on how we relate to others and how we respond to particular events in our lives. People who do not feel that they are worthwhile usually express their frustrations and insecurities in their interactions with others.

There is an epidemic in our society today called "blame." People blame others and the circumstances in their lives for how they feel and for what happens to them. "He made me feel angry" is an often-heard statement made by many students. Children respond to external events as though they have no control over their feelings. They blame others for the way they feel.

What happens is that children become robots. They develop negative patterns of thought in response to external events, which lead to negative feelings and emotions, which contribute to poor human relations. It's as if they're on "automatic" when responding. Someone calls them a name and they respond by acting out, becoming involved in an argument, or even worse–a fight. When the children are asked why they became involved in the fight they say, "He made me mad, so I hit him!" Or their feelings get hurt due to what they perceive to be a negative event. In response the children withdraw, creating an isolating result.

Here is the cause-and-effect relationship that takes place with a perceived negative event.

An Event, which is out of a child's direct control, brings about

Perception of the Event, which is within a child's control, brings about

Self-Talk, which is within a child's control, brings about

Feelings, which are out of a child's direct control, bring about

Behavior, which is out of a child's direct control, produces

A Result, or the circumstances of life.

GA1501

Better Behavior = Better Results

Goal: Students will accept responsibility for their current situations. Students will begin to understand that external events have no attached meaning.

Time: 40 minutes

Setting: Classroom

Materials: Better Behavior = Better Results work sheets

Procedure:

1. First write "Event + Behavior = Results" on the board.

2. Explain to the children: "An event might be, for example, a ball flies across the playground accidentally hitting a person in the head. That person's behavior to this event might be that he gets really angry and decides to pick up the ball, kick it over the fence, and push the player who was only trying to catch the ball. The result might be that the two kids get into a fight and then are suspended."

3. Explain: "Most of the time we complain about the bad things that happen in our lives; these are the results. Adults complain about many things and so do kids. Kids complain about being yelled at by their parents or about what others did to them on the playground or about getting a bad grade on their report card. These things that we complain about are the results of our life. What happens is that an event takes place and then our behavior is added (+) and together this equals (=) the results. In our example, the event is the ball hitting a boy in the head, the boy's behavior is kicking the ball over the fence and pushing the other person, and the result is a fight that gets both kids suspended."

4. Write the example on the board:

Event	+	Behavior	=	Result
Ball hits boy in the head		Boy kicks the ball and pushes the kid		Fight and suspension

5. Continue explaining: "Here's another example. It's report card time and students are getting their grades. The teacher is passing out the report cards, and there are two kids who are getting the very same grade in math. Both Joe and Sally are receiving a D in math this time on their report cards. Joe looks at his grade, is very unhappy, and decides that it's all the teacher's fault. Joe decides that the teacher just doesn't like him and that's why he got the D. Sally, on the other hand, looks at her grade, is very unhappy, and decides that she was the one who just didn't try or work hard enough to get a better grade."

6. Continue explaining: "Joe decides that he doesn't like the teacher now because she gave him a bad grade. So Joe does even less math work and doesn't even try to do a good job on the work that he does complete. But Sally decides that she is responsible for her grade. So Sally starts to try harder and asks more questions, she does extra credit work in math, and also studies harder at home. Later, because of Joe's behavior, the next time the report cards come out he receives an F. And because of Sally's behavior, the next time the report cards come out she receives a B."

GA1501

7. Illustrate Joe's equation:

Teacher asks: "So, for Joe what was the event?"
Children answer: "Joe received a D in math."
Teacher asks: "What was his behavior?"
Children answer: "He blamed his grade on the teacher, got angry, and didn't do any more math work."
Teacher asks: "What was the result?"
Children answer: "Joe received an F in math on his next report card."

Event	+	Behavior	=	Result
Joe received a D in math		Joe wouldn't do any more math work.		Joe received an F on his next report card.

8. Illustrate Sally's equation:

Teacher asks: "Good job! Now, what about Sally? What was the event there?"
Children answer: "Sally received a D in math."
Teacher asks: "What was her behavior?"
Children answer: "She decided to try harder and did extra credit math work."
Teacher asks: "What was the result?"
Children answer: "Sally received a B in math on her next report card."

Event	+	Behavior	=	Result
Sally received a D in math		She worked harder and did extra credit math work.		Sally received a B on her next report card.

9. Then ask: "Who do you think produced the better result?" Students answer, "Sally did!" Continue explaining, "That's right! Sally simply behaved differently to the very same event. And because of her different behavior, Sally produced a better result than Joe. What we do most of the time is hope that the events in our life will be different. We usually hear this when people say, 'If only the other kids would like me better. If only my mom were more understanding. If only my teacher could see me doing better things. If only . . . If only . . . If only . . .' But, most of the time those events aren't the exact way we want them to be. Sure, sometimes they are, but sometimes they're not. If we want to have a different or better result, we will need to have a better behavior."

"If Joe wanted a different result on his report card maybe he could change his behavior in the room by thinking, 'I'd like to do something quite a bit different. Maybe if I decided to work harder and ask for help more often I could get a better grade.' If we want something else different on our report card or from our teacher, mother, or friends, we're going to have to behave a little differently to get a better result. If you want a better result, sometimes you'll need to change your behavior."

GA1501

10. In conclusion, explain: "The Event + Behavior = Result equation helps us to understand that if we want to change things for the better, we need to stop blaming the event or the other people. Instead we should take responsibility for our lives every moment of the day. We can start to think about our own behavior. Once we do this we start to produce the kind of results we really want."

11. Finally, pass out the Better Behavior = Better Results work sheets. Ask student volunteers to role-play the various situations, and then decide on the Better Behaviors and Better Results to be written in the appropriate spaces.

GA1501

Better Behavior = Better Results

If you want better results it takes a little bit of **practice** to find the best behavior. With your teacher's help pick people to role-play these different behaviors to see if you can have a better result.

Example:

Event +	**Behavior** =	**Result**
A project that you worked on for a long time accidentally gets knocked off a table and breaks.	You get angry and shove the person who accidentally knocked over your project.	You get sent to the principal's office and receive a detention.

Same Event +	**Better Behavior** =	**Better Result**
A project that you worked on for a long time accidentally gets knocked off a table and breaks.	You listen while your classmate explains how your project was accidently bumped.	You and your classmate work together to fix your project.

There! It looks as good as new!

GA1501

Your turn.

#1

Event +	**Behavior** =	**Result**
Your classmates start a game of kickball without you.	You think to yourself that they don't like you, so you go sit down alone on the other side of the playground.	You don't get invited to play in other games with your classmates.

Same Event +	**Better Behavior** =	**Better Result**
Your classmates start a game of kickball without you.	_____ _____ _____ _____ _____	You make a friend and start a new game together the next day at recess.

#2

Event +	**Behavior** =	**Result**
You look inside your desk and notice that your pencil is missing.	You blame all your table partners and accuse them of stealing your pencil.	Your table partners don't ask you to play with them on your free time period.

Same Event +	**Better Behavior** =	**Better Result**
You look inside your desk and notice that your pencil is missing.	_____ _____ _____ _____	_____ _____ _____ _____

GA1501

Become a "Star"

Goal: Students will acquire a cognitive organizer to help control their behavior in regard to particular events in their lives.
Time: 20-30 minutes
Setting: Classroom
Materials: Poster board, pencils, and markers or crayons
Procedure: Start by writing the letters on the chalkboard: S T A R.

Explain that:

The "S" stands for STOP.
The "T" stands for THINK.
The "A" stands for AWARE.
The "R" stands for RESPOND.

Explain to your students: "Events happen in our lives that we behave automatically to. Sometimes we get into trouble or feel badly about ourselves because of the way we think about those events. If we slow down or stop our thinking, we can produce better results. We can become STARs."

Continue explaining: "For example Tony goes up to Quincy and says, 'Your haircut looks stupid!' Quincy can now either react automatically with a comment to try to make Tony feel bad, like, 'At least I'm not as ugly as you!' That might just start a fight. Or Quincy could just stop and think about why Tony would say a thing like that. 'Gee, maybe Tony doesn't feel that good about himself, so he has to try to put me down.' Now Quincy is aware of the real problem and he can respond in a way that will not create a fight. Perhaps Quincy doesn't 'feed in' to Tony's problem and decides to just walk away."

Continue explaining: "So the next time that you find yourself involved in a situation where you hear a put-down from someone, first, take the time to Stop (don't react). Then Think: What is that person telling you about him- or herself? Why did the person say what he or she said? Next become Aware of whose problem it really is and how you feel. Finally, Respond in a way that doesn't take away power from anyone.

Conclude by saying: "If this isn't the way you handle a situation, there is always the opposite way of responding. If you do that, then you're all a bunch of RATS!"

Finally have several of your students construct a poster or bulletin board with the words *Stop, Think, Aware, Respond*. Maybe they can illustrate an example of students using the STAR technique.

119

GA1501

Journal Writing for Determining a Purpose

To have a purpose, a child must be encouraged to dream, to think big, and to have an ambition. It also means planning what one must do to realize that goal. The following sentence stems are designed with that purpose in mind.

- When I become an adult I'm going to . . .

- The most important thing I'm going to do is . . .

- For me to do well in school, I will need to . . .

- This week I plan to . . .

- Someday I hope to . . .

- The best way to solve a problem is to . . .

- I would like to learn all about . . .

- When I reach my goals I feel . . .

- My dream is to someday become . . .

- When I get home from school today, I am going to . . .

- On my next report card I plan to . . .

- I am very good at . . .

- I wish school was . . .

- I want to be a . . .

- If I could go anywhere in the world, I would . . .

- My goal for this week is to . . .

- I will make this school year a . . .

- I can help out at home by . . .

- Sometimes I dream about . . .

- I would like to get better at . . .

- I will reach my goals by . . .

- Today I am going to . . .

- If I were in charge of this school, I would . . .

- Setting goals helps me to . . .

- One thing I would like to change about myself is . . .

- When I don't make my goal, I feel . . .

- For my next recess I would like to . . .

- When I go to high school I will . . .

- If I were in charge of the world, I would . . .

- If I were granted three wishes, I would . . .

GA1501

Interdisciplinary Activities

Social Science

The Railroad

Goal: Students will understand how communities depend on the railroad for goods and services.

Time: Several days

Setting: Classroom

Materials: Suggestions include cardboard boxes, tagboard, construction paper, markers, or whatever you and your students need. (Activity choice will determine.)

Procedure: Studying transportation, trains, and the railroad will provide a myriad of activity ideas that you and your students will be able to generate–starting a railroad company by having students choose various roles, such as workers, train cars, passengers to ride in a passenger train, or possibly even different types of goods and materials such as cows, automobiles, or furniture to ride in a freight car. Have students get in line as a "human train," with their hands on one another's shoulders. Then have the train travel to a predetermined destination. Make sure the train is making "choo-choo" sounds while traveling along its tracks! Different types of train cars and railroad jobs to research are listed below.

Workers:

Conductor: Captain of the train, he watches over passengers and crew.

Brakeman: Helps conductor with safe operation of train. Uncouple cars.

Engineer: Runs the locomotive and is responsible for its speeds, signals, and safety.

Pullman: Collects reservations.

Porter: Works in sleeper cars to help make people comfortable.

Chef: Top person in kitchen.

Waiter: Serves guests.

Cars:

Railcar: The engine car

Hopper Car: Hauls bulk freight like coal, etc.

Flatcar: Hauls big and long materials such as timber.

Cattle Car: Hauls cows, sheep, pigs, etc.

Piggyback Car: Hauls truck trailers.

Gondola Car: Hauls metal products and bulk freight.

Auto Car: Hauls cars and trucks.

Boxcar: Carries general freight like boxes, etc.

Tank Car: Carries oil and other liquids.

Refrigerator Car: Carries meat, frozen foods, and other perishables.

Caboose: Last car on train serving as office for the conductor.

Pullman Car: Carries passengers.

GA1501

Music

Railroad Songs

Goal: Students will be willing to participate in musical experiences from different historical sources.
Time: 10-15 minutes
Setting: Classroom
Materials: Copies of the songs
Procedure: Students love singing traditional railroad and train songs. Try singing them while you're working on a project!

Down by the Station

Down by the station, early in the morning
See the little puffer bellies, all in a row.
See the station master, pull a little handle
Chug! Chug! Toot! Toot! Off we go!

I've Been Workin' on the Railroad

I've been workin' on the railroad
All the live long day.
I've been workin' on the railroad
Just to pass the time away.
Don't you hear the whistle blowin'?
Rise up so early in the morn,
Don't you hear the captain shoutin',
"Dinah, blow your horn"?

Physical Education

Railroad Relay

Goal: Students will give their best effort and practice good sportsmanship to reach group goals.
Time: 20 minutes
Setting: Playground
Materials: Start and finish line, cones or classroom chairs
Procedure: Divide your class into teams with five or six members. Have your student teams line up behind the starting line. Then have them place their hands on the shoulders of the person in front of them. Tell them that now each group has become a train. Make sure they know which of them is the railcar and which is the caboose! Then explain that each train is to hop down to and around the cone or chair on the other end of the playground and return to the start/finish line to win the relay. On the command, "Train Track," they are to go! Make sure they are hopping or students may trip on one another's feet.

Toys, Toys, Toys

The Little Blue Engine had to pull many different toys over the mountain. Match the words with the proper toys.

doll   jackknife   sailboat   books
kite   toy engine   picture puzzle   top
book   board game   fire truck   clown

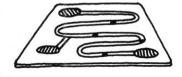

_____   _____   _____

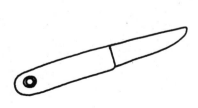

_____   _____   _____

_____   _____   _____

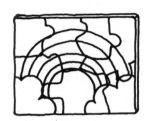

_____   _____   _____

Good Things to Eat

The Little Blue Engine carried many good things for the girls and boys on the other side of the mountain to eat. Match the words to the drawings. Write the words on the lines below the drawings.

big golden oranges
red-cheeked apples
bottles of creamy milk

fresh spinach
peppermints
lollipops

_____

_____

_____

_____

_____

_____

Thank You, Little Blue Engine

The Little Blue Engine worked very hard to get the toys over the mountain. He decided that he MUST get the toys to the children on the other side of the mountain. Pretend you are one of those children and write a thank-you letter to the Little Engine That Could.

_____
(today's date)

_____
(your street address)

Dear Little Blue Engine,

_____

_____

_____

_____

_____

_____

Sincerely,

_____
(your name)

In the Right Order?

Number the pictures in the way they happened in *The Little Engine That Could*. Write the number below the picture.

The toys ask the Freight Engine for help.

_____

The toys ask the Passenger Engine for help.

_____

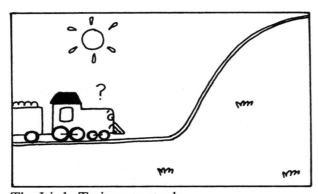

The Little Train gets stuck.

_____

The toys ask the Little Blue Engine for help.

_____

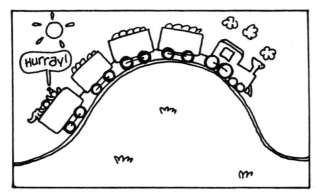

The Little Blue Engine pulls the toys over the mountain.

_____

The toys ask the Rusty Old Engine for help.

_____

GA1501

Yes, I Can . . .

The Little Blue Engine said, "I think I can. I think I can." Think of all the things you can do. What's that? You mean you're having a hard time thinking of all the things you can do? Aw, come on! Can you tie your shoes? Can you jump in a puddle? Can you turn on the TV? I'll bet you can! I'll bet you can think! I'll bet you can think of a few more things you CAN DO!

I can _____

I can be a _____

I can have a _____

I can do a _____

I can learn to _____

I can think of _____

I can write about_____

I can talk about_____

I can dream about_____

**Looks like you
can do a lot!**

127

GA1501

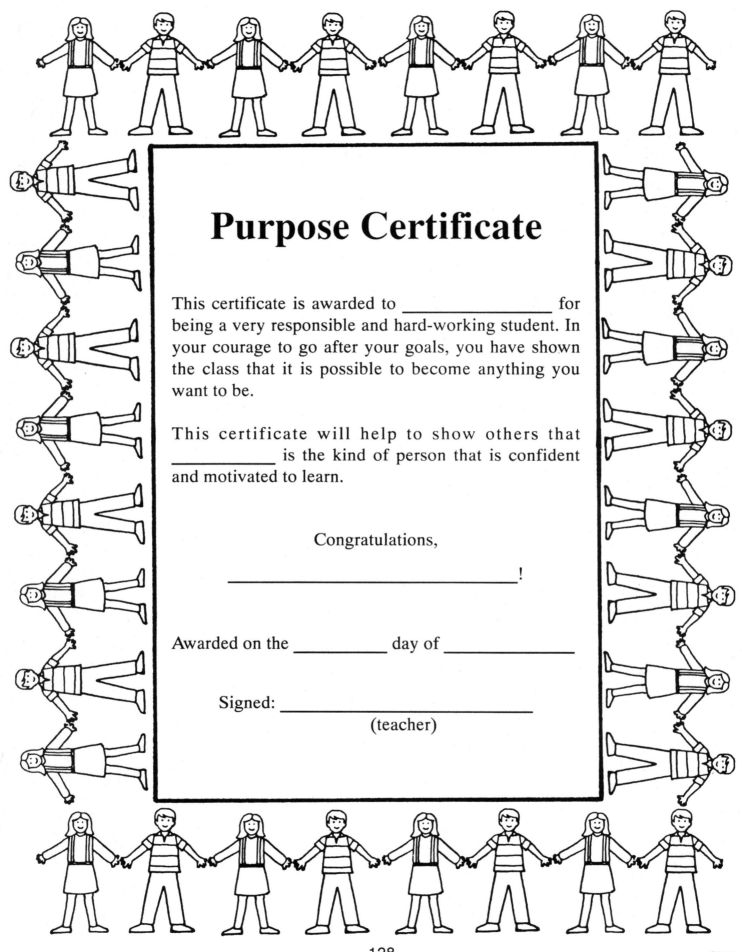

Purpose Certificate

This certificate is awarded to _____ for being a very responsible and hard-working student. In your courage to go after your goals, you have shown the class that it is possible to become anything you want to be.

This certificate will help to show others that _____ is the kind of person that is confident and motivated to learn.

Congratulations,

_____!

Awarded on the _____ day of _____

Signed: _____
(teacher)

GA1501

Promoting Competence

"The reward of a thing well done is to have done it."
– Ralph Waldo Emerson

A Winning Attitude

When students have experienced frequent successes they begin to take notice of their strengths and abilities. They have acquired a list of positive accomplishments that reminds them that they are capable and competent. Students begin to develop a winning attitude that carries them through future challenges in life. Students will feel confident about their own ability to perform, and they expect to do well, continuing to strive. Looking forward to new experiences, knowing that they will be able to learn the next task and eventually do it well is a characteristic of students who have learned competence. These children understand that it is okay to make mistakes because mistakes are only opportunities for learning. And they understand that all they have to do after making a mistake is make some minor adjustments in their actions, and they will eventually produce a successful outcome. Feeling competent is something that can be learned!

Promoting Competence with *Oh, the Places You'll Go!*

My favorite Dr. Seuss book of all time is the farfetched story of a little boy successfully traveling through the trials and tribulations of an adventurous life. In *Oh, the Places You'll Go!* right away you know that this kid is off to great places; he's "off and away!" We learn that life has its ups and downs, we can expect the best of times, and also because of a mistake, sometimes the worst. We learn that sometimes we'll be alone, sometimes our own worst enemy, and sometimes we'll end up in that awful place–the waiting place. But then we'll confront our problems, solve them, and escape to be on our way again!

> "And will you succeed?
> Yes! You will, indeed!
> (98 and $^3/_4$% guaranteed.)
> KID, YOU'LL MOVE MOUNTAINS!" [1]

Oh, the Places You'll Go! provides us with a terrific way to lead into Roald Dahl's book, *James and the Giant Peach.* Perhaps you'll want to have everyone in the class read his or her own copy or maybe you'll want to read the story to the class yourself. Either way it creates a great introduction to the theme of experiencing competence.

---

1. From OH, THE PLACES YOU'LL GO! by Dr. Seuss. Copyright © 1990 by Audrey S. Geisel and Karl ZoBell, trustees under the trust agreement dated August 27, 1984. Reprinted by permission of Random House, Inc.

Promoting Competence with *James and the Giant Peach*

In *James and the Giant Peach*, James Henry Trotter, one of the saddest and loneliest boys in the whole world, lives with his two wicked aunts, Aunt Sponge and Aunt Spiker. All three of them live in a ramshackle house high on a hill in the south of England. One day James meets a strange little man who gives him a bag of green crystals. The strange little man tells James to mix them in water and drink them, and if he does, he will never be miserable again. Fortunately, because of his obvious excitement, James runs towards the house and trips, and all of the magic crystals disappear into the ground right under the old peach tree. Too bad for James! But in no time at all an enormous peach, bigger than a house, grows on the tree. One night James discovers a door on the side of the peach and decides to go in. He finds six enormous creatures that have apparently been waiting for him. The next morning one of the creatures gnaws off the stem of the peach and the enormous peach proceeds to roll down the hill, killing the wicked aunts. Yeaaa! The peach is on a mad roll down to the sea. Now the adventure begins! Confronted with a variety of obstacles, James saves the peach and the enormous insects again and again until they finally reach the eastern coastline of America. The peach finally lands on the pinnacle of the Empire State Building and everyone aboard becomes a hero!

"And thus the journey ended. But the travelers lived on. Everyone of them became rich and successful in the new country.

"And James Henry Trotter, who once, if you remember, had been the saddest and loneliest little boy that you could find, now had all the playmates in the world. And because so many of them were always begging him to tell and tell again the story of his adventures on the peach, he thought it would be nice if one day he sat down and wrote it as a book. So he did. And that is what you have just finished reading." [1]

James learns competence by making decisions and taking action. And if he makes a mistake (which isn't very often), he learns from the experience, resets his goal, takes a different course of action, and celebrates his success.

Thematic Unit:	Competence
Core Literature:	*Oh, the Places You'll Go!* by Dr. Seuss (Random House)
	James and the Giant Peach by Roald Dahl (Knopf)
Extended Literature:	*Stone Fox* by John Reynolds Gardiner (Harper & Row)
Recreational Literature:	Other books by Dr. Seuss and Roald Dahl

---

1. From JAMES AND THE GIANT PEACH by Roald Dahl. Copyright © 1961 and renewed 1989 by Roald Dahl. Reprinted by permission of Alfred A. Knopf, Inc.

Additional Literature Supporting the Theme of Competence

Adam of the Road by Elizabeth Gray (Viking)
By the Great Horn Spoon by Sid Fleischman (Little, Brown)
Dragonwings by Laurence Yep (Cornerstone Books)
From the Mixed Up Files of Mrs. Basil E. Frankweiler by E. Konigsburg (Atheneum)
Good-Bye, My Wishing Star by Vicki Grove
Henry Reed, Inc. by Keith Robertson (Viking Press)
I Have a Dream: The Story of Martin Luther King by Margaret Davidson (Scholastic)
The Indian in the Cupboard by Lynne Reid Banks (Avon)
Island of the Blue Dolphins by Scott O'Dell (Houghton Mifflin)
Legend of the Paintbrush by Tomie de Paola (G.P. Putnam's Sons)
Love You Forever by Robert Munsch (Firefly Books)
Misty of Chincoteague by Marguerite Henry (Macmillan Publishing Co.)
Mrs. Frisby and the Rats of NIMH by Robert O'Brien (Atheneum)
My Side of the Mountain by Jean Craighead George (Dutton)
Sadako and the Thousand Paper Cranes by Eleanor Coerr (Dell)
Save Queen of Sheba by Louise Moeri (Avon)
Sign of the Beaver by Elizabeth Speare (Houghton Mifflin)
Three Little Pigs by Paul Galdone (Clarion Books/Houghton Mifflin)
The Wright Brothers at Kitty Hawk by Donald J. Sobol (Scholastic)

Supporting Subthemes of Competence

The following subthemes help to support or complement promoting competence, the final step of enhancing self-esteem. Subthemes provide a tangent for either the teacher or the students to take when developing understanding of the theme of competence.

- Government
- Justice
- Power
- Quality
- Wisdom
- Wealth
- Determination
- Strength
- Autonomy

- Infinity
- Peace
- Law
- Liberty
- Life
- Significance
- Perseverance
- Empowerment

- Risk
- Failure
- Success
- Competence
- Capability
- Intelligence
- Authority
- Independence

Self-Esteem Theme Objectives

The teacner will . . .

1. **Provide opportunities for students to explore interests freely**. By being sensitive to students' interests we promote curiosity and self-direction. When children control their learning they are much more motivated and as a result, performance increases. I think we can all agree that we do well in our areas of personal interest. When we structure a learning environment that allows children to discover and explore their interests, they become more aware of personal strengths and competencies.

131

GA1501

2. Teach children how to recognize and acknowledge personal achievement. Students must eventually learn how to generate their own self-esteem. We will not always be there to praise them and tell them how well they are doing. When students are able to recognize their achievements and praise themselves for those achievements, then initiative, competence and mastery continue to build.

3. Teach students how to learn from their mistakes. Teach students to understand the causes of events, to make plans and anticipate consequences, direct their attention to the relevant details of a problem, and, rather than impose solutions, encourage children to solve problems themselves. By providing specific feedback without actually solving the problem itself, we assist children in considering alternatives towards improvement. Children learn to actually profit from their mistakes. Remember, it takes both rain and sunshine to make a rainbow!

4. Incorporate envisioneering techniques. Children can be taught to creatively imagine their future moving in a positive direction. Envisioneering experiences provided by the classroom teacher will help children improve their performance and build ambition.

The students will . . .

• Develop a feeling of success and accomplishment in pursuits that they consider worthwhile.
• Become aware of strengths and become able to accept weaknesses.

GA1501

Code of Conduct

Goal: Students will become aware of their own self-importance and increase the acceptance of others.

Time: Varies depending on the extent of instruction

Setting: Classroom

Materials: Tagboard and markers

Procedure: I know it's hard to believe, but the following statements comprised the Scandinavian Code of Conduct in 1933. Check it out.

> Don't think that you are anything special.
> Don't think that you are as much as we.
> Don't think that you are wiser than we.
> Don't think that you know more than we do.
> Don't think that you are capable.
> Don't think that anyone cares for you as an individual.

Can you believe it? I wonder who "we" is? I sure hope it wasn't a teacher.

In 1992 a teacher decided to do something about this mess. At the First International Self-Esteem Conference in Oslo, Norway, an educator devised a new Code of Conduct. Thank goodness! Here it is.

> I am unique.
> I have a value that no one can measure.
> I can contribute something that is special.
> I have enormous potential.
> I have done much to be proud of.
> I am lovable and capable.
> I have much to give others.
> I accept others the way they are.
> I can understand and learn from others.
> I know that some people love me.

Personally, I prefer the new Code of Conduct that the modern-day teacher wrote. The new statements are actually affirmations that make for a great oral language exercise. Perhaps you could have the students recite these statements daily.

Another great idea is to have the students draw pictures that represent each of the statements. Make posters of the drawings and statements. Hang the posters up on the walls in the classroom.

Self-Esteem Pledge of Allegiance

Goal: Students will understand that each person has dignity and worth. Students will exhibit pride and respect for one's self.

Time: Every day, right after the Pledge of Allegiance to the Flag

Setting: Classroom

Materials: One piece of tagboard and markers

Procedure: Every morning we recite the Pledge of Allegiance to the flag in our elementary classrooms. I personally believe this to be a worthwhile task. But what about having allegiance to ourselves? What about being loyal to ourselves, standing by our beliefs, and being guided by our own inner voices?

After the pledge to the flag, try a pledge of allegiance to ourselves. It makes a great oral language exercise at the beginning of the day. While you're at it maybe you could make a great vocabulary lesson out of it as well. And you can take the meanings of these words with the children as far as you want to.

Allegiance (noun) 1: loyalty and obedience owed to one's country or government 2: loyalty or devotion to some person, group, or cause.

Dignity (noun) 1: the quality or state of being worthy, honored, or esteemed 2: high rank, position or office.

Honor (noun) 1: good name; public esteem: REPUTATION: a showing of usually merited respect.

Pride (noun) 1: the quality or state of being proud: a reasonable or justifiable self-respect: pleasure or satisfaction taken in some act, accomplishment, or possession.

These words can be pretty heavy if you really consider them. Do you and your students practice these concepts? Here's the pledge.

**I pledge allegiance to myself and all that I can be.
And to myself for which I stand,
one person under God, with Dignity, Honor, and Pride.**

GA1501

Code of Persistence

Goal: Students will realize that at times several attempts or continued effort may be necessary to attain goals.

Time: Several days or every morning for oral reading

Setting: Classroom

Materials: One piece of tagboard

Procedure: Have you ever noticed how some kids seem to give up easily on tasks that may take a little longer than they thought they would? Well, part of promoting competence means becoming a little tenacious. Calvin Coolidge once said,

"Nothing in the world can take the place of persistence. Talent will not, nothing is more common than unsuccessful men with talent. Genius will not, unrewarded genius is almost a proverb. Education will not, the world is full of educated derelicts. Persistence and determination alone are omnipotent."

Children develop "stick-to-itiveness" as they grow older. But it never hurts, I think, to encourage them to stay with a task. This exercise helps to remind kids that it takes effort to acquire something of value. Plus, when incorporated as an oral language exercise from time to time, the kids memorize it and have a good time doing it as well.

Have one child shout out the numbers as the class recites the sentence afterward. For example, one student loudly says, "Number 1!" Then the rest of the class says, "I will never . . . !" And so on, and so on, until you're done.

Number 1: I will never give up so long as I know I am right.

Number 2: I will believe that all things will work out for me if I hang on until the end.

Number 3: I will be courageous and undismayed in the face of odds.

Number 4: I will not permit anyone to intimidate me or deter me from my goals.

Number 5: I will fight to overcome all handicaps and setbacks.

Number 6: I will try again and again to accomplish what I desire.

Number 7: I will take new faith and resolution from the knowledge that all successful people have had to fight defeat.

Number 8: I will never surrender to discouragement or despair no matter what obstacles may confront me.

– Herman Sherman

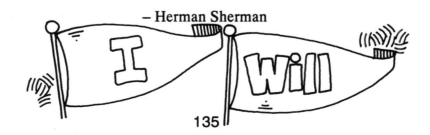

GA1501

The Pluses About Me

Goal: Students will understand the components that enhance a person's sense of self-esteem and will describe behaviors and characteristics of persons who have positive self-esteem.

Time: One hour

Setting: Classroom

Materials: Work sheet entitled "The Pluses About Me"

Procedure:

1. Write the term *Self-Esteem* on the chalkboard and state, "Believing in one's own value as a person is the most important part of being a healthy person." Explain, "The word *esteem* means the same as worth or value." Then ask the class, "What do you think the word self-esteem means?" Write their answers on the board. Then explain, "Self-esteem is the worth or respect people have for their qualities, characteristics, what they can do, how they look, and their accomplishments." Continue explaining, "The way we think about our characteristics may be good or bad. That means that the way we think about ourselves may help us or harm us, may make us feel good about ourselves or bad about ourselves. The more you like your characteristics, the higher your self-esteem. The more you don't like your characteristics, the lower your self-esteem. Your self-esteem determines the worth, respect, and value you feel about yourself and also the worth or value you feel about other people. High self-esteem helps you to appreciate your characteristics and those in other people as well. Knowing what your abilities are and believing in them gives you the confidence to learn new things, to make good choices and decisions, and to improve those things you would like to change."

2. Explain, "Low self-esteem often is bad for your confidence and your ability to succeed. If you lack self-confidence and are afraid of doing badly, this will prevent you from knowing what your good qualities are, and also being able to tell what good qualities other people have. If you have low self-esteem you may not try very hard to learn something new. You may not try to do your best. When you have low self-esteem, you may even cut down what you do and be happy when other people fail."

3. Ask your students, "Who are some people that you know or have seen on television that you think have high self-esteem?" List their responses on the board. Then write the two categories "High Self-Esteem" and "Low Self-Esteem" on the board. Next ask your students, "What are the characteristics of people who have high self-esteem?" Write their responses. "And what are the characteristics of people who have low self-esteem?" Write their answers.

4. Then explain, "Developing high self-esteem is something you do all your life. The feelings that we have about our own achievements and failures and also the way others feel about us have an influence on our self-esteem. We are forever growing and learning, and sometimes it takes time to learn to like our good qualities and to accept the changes that are a normal part of growing up. Sometimes things that young people don't like about themselves when they're young may turn out to be those things which they are very happy about when they get older. For instance, someone may not like being very tall when in fifth grade, but then when that person gets older, he or she may like being tall."

5. Explain to students, "The first step in having high self-esteem is to know what is good about ourselves." Then say, "One thing I like about myself is _____." Then say, "That was a little hard, but I did it. Now what are some things you like about yourself?" Take the time to go around to each student to share with the class at least one thing that is likable about him- or herself. If someone isn't able to think of anything, ask the other students to help.

6. Finally, pass out the work sheet "The Pluses About Me" and explain the instructions to the students. Take the time to fill out the answers yourself. When everyone is finished, discuss what was written. Maybe some of the students will be willing to share their answers with the class.

GA1501

The Pluses About Me

Directions: Fill in the blanks below to show the way you think and feel about yourself.

1. These are the things I do well:

( ) _____

( ) _____

( ) _____

2. These are the things that are important to me:

( ) _____

( ) _____

( ) _____

3. These are the things that I like about myself:

( ) _____

( ) _____

( ) _____

4. These are the subjects I enjoy most in school:

( ) _____

( ) _____

( ) _____

5. These are the subjects I enjoy least in school:

( ) _____

( ) _____

( ) _____

Good! Okay, now that you have done all that, the next step is to go back and put a plus sign (+) inside of the parentheses ( ) by the things you do really well. Also put a minus sign (-) inside of the parentheses ( ) by the things that you would like to improve. Then count up the total plus and minus signs and write the numbers below.

_____ Total Plus Marks   _____ Total Minus Marks

Do you have more plus signs or more minus signs? _____

What do you think that means? _____

_____

On a scale of one to ten, with one being the lowest and ten being the highest, where do you think your self-esteem is right now? Circle the number that best describes you.

1 2 3 4 5 6 7 8 9 10

Where would you like your self-esteem to be?

1 2 3 4 5 6 7 8 9 10

GA1501

Envisioneering Activities

Envisioneering is a very powerful tool that will improve a student's performance and self-esteem. By providing children with envisioneering experiences, where children creatively imagine a positive future or self, we can facilitate the enhancement of their self-esteem.

All of us carry an image in our mind that represents our self or how we will perform a particular task in the future. These images have a profound impact on the way we actually experience the world. A good indicator of positive self-esteem is the "Possible Self," or ambition that we hold for our future. Where we think our "Possible Self" will be in the future, whether it be involved in gangs and drugs, or as a successful doctor, lawyer or teacher, is also indicative of what we think of ourself in the present. Helping children to improve their "self-image" will improve their self-esteem in the present and their chances for a positive future. Forming mental images in the "mind's eye" and the visual perception of an actual experience are exactly similar events to the brain. Whatever a student can picture in his or her mind, he or she can achieve. Feeling the effect, whether real or imagined, of accomplishing any goal will help motivate students to make it a reality.

Learning and the Brain

Learning occurs throughout the entire brain. Research has shown that the brain has two halves or hemispheres, the right and left. Each hemisphere processes different types of information.

Left Hemisphere	Right Hemisphere
Sequential, time-oriented tasks	Space-oriented tasks
Facts, lists, and computations	Images, pictures, and metaphors
Logical thinking	Holistic thinking
Verbal tasks	Nonverbal tasks
Rational	Intuitive
Linear	Feeling

These processes can't really be assigned to only the right or left hemisphere because learning occurs throughout the entire brain; however, education has favored one type of teaching–a sequential, factual, linear, and verbal process.

When both modes of hemispheric processing operate simultaneously, sometimes genius results. Albert Einstein discovered his famous theory of relativity in this very same way. One day while lying under a tree, the young Albert began playing with the beams of sunlight as they flickered through his eyelashes. He visualized what it would be like to travel on a beam of light, and as his mind wandered with that image, he had an insight of exactly what it would be like.

Albert Einstein used both hemispheres of his brain simultaneously, mixing visual images with his technical background. One way to facilitate the utilization of the whole brain is to present an envisioneering experience, followed by a writing assignment, art project, or verbal description of the experience. Who knows, maybe you'll discover some real genius in your classroom!

GA1501

Introducing Envisioneering Activities

1. Begin with a discussion about dreams and daydreams.
2. Ask the children to close their eyes and open them as fast as possible. Sometimes children are apprehensive about closing their eyes. Ask, "What do we call it when we close our eyes that fast?" Answer, "Blinking!" "Now can you close your eyes for a longer time?"
3. Ask the children if they can close their eyes and see their favorite animal. Ask, "What kind of animal did you see?" Discuss the animals and ask, "Why did we all see different kinds of animals?" One student told me, as if she thought I was stupid for asking such a question, "Because we all have different brains, gosh!"
4. Now you're ready to start with an envisioneering experience. But say to the class, "I'd like to try something a little different with you now, but I'm not sure you're ready for it." Chances are the class will beg you for the experience.

Classroom Environment

The classroom should feel safe, comfortable, and relaxed. Close the doors, turn down the lights, explain to the children to raise their hands if they have a concern, allow no talking, and state that there will be no grades given for the experience. Perhaps some very relaxing music the children enjoy could be playing.

Student Condition

Students should be relaxed and calm. Sometimes it is best to allow the children the opportunity to expend some energy before beginning the envisioneering experience so that they are able to relax the whole time. Once started have the children sit in a way so that very little movement is necessary. Perhaps they can sit with both feet flat on the ground and with the hands palm down on the desk. Have the children concentrate on the sounds in the room first, and then have them concentrate on their bodily functions (breathing, cold air in through the nostrils, warm air out the mouth, chest rising and falling, etc.).

The Experience

1. It's important to remember to make the experience as real as possible for the participants. When leading the children through the envisioneering experience, you want to bring into play as many of the modalities as possible: visual, auditory, kinesthetic, and olfactory. "See the large twisting tree, hear the wind through the branches, feel the rough bark, and smell the earthy aroma."
2. Facilitators should remember to use a calm voice and pace their speech.
3. When a distraction enters the experience, just acknowledge it and move on. "Be aware of the knock on the door, but continue to concentrate."
4. Use both structured experiences, where you guide everything that happens in the experience, and unstructured experiences, where you allow the children to guide themselves through a portion of the experience.
5. When completing the envisioneering experience it's important to direct the children to completion slowly. This can be done by counting, and at the end of the count the children open their eyes, or by slowly guiding their awareness to the room environment, or by helping them to be aware of their bodies once again (breathing, feeling their backs up against the backs of the chairs, etc.).

GA1501

Extension

Afterward it is important for the children to link the envisioneering experience together with an activity that emphasizes the converse mode of hemispheric processing–namely, the "left brain." The activity will allow the child to ground the experience and remember it. The extension activity can be accomplished in many forms, to accommodate a variety of learning styles. Some suggestions are writing, drawing, discussion, sculpting, movement, and affirming declarations. Some questions for discussion are "What did you do? See? Hear? Feel? Learn?" "What are you going to do now?" "How can you use this in your everyday life?"

"Some men see things as they are and say 'Why?'
I dream things that never were and say 'Why not?'"

– George Bernard Shaw

"The most pathetic person in the world is someone who has sight but has no vision."

– Helen Keller

GA1501

Envisioneering Experience #1: The Hero Within

Goal: Students will recognize qualities within themselves to reduce stress and anxiety, gaining respect of self and obtaining personal satisfaction.

Time: 20 minutes (This activity will take longer if the extension activity is utilized.)

Setting: Classroom

Materials: None, unless your students complete a drawing or write about their experience. For the drawing you will need construction paper, crayons, markers, paper, and pencils.

Procedure: Children enjoy having a personal mentor or hero figure in their lives, someone who will stand up for them, give them advice, and protect them. This mentor may take many forms, a stuffed animal, imaginary older friend, or grandparent. An example of this is the relationship that a little boy has with his stuffed tiger in the comic strip, "Calvin and Hobbes." Little Calvin is always talking to and getting advice from his confidant Hobbes. Calvin doesn't always listen, but nonetheless they have a very special relationship.

Children build special relationships with their personal "heroes" through the use of envisioneering. When the hero comes from within, children discover that they have qualities inside themselves that they can draw on as tools for everyday living. The children learn that they have courage, power, understanding, and strength.

Here is how our "hero" helps us:

Close your eyes and concentrate on your breath going in and out of your nostrils. Notice how relaxed you are as you continue to concentrate on your breathing. Imagine that you are walking on a path in a very thick forest. You notice that all around you are big, beautiful, green trees. The air feels cool and calm. As you walk down this path toward the sound of running water you come upon a small stream. Walk over to the stream and look at your reflection in the water. (Pause.) All at once you notice something or someone standing next to you, and you feel completely comfortable and safe. You see another reflection next to your own in the water. This other being could be a wise old person, an animal, or an imaginary friend. You know that this being is someone whom you can trust, someone you have known for a very long time. This special being signals for you to follow across a small bridge that crosses the stream. You follow and after crossing the stream both of you start climbing a hill that leads to a cave. You and your friend enter the cave and sit down. While in the cave your friend begins to tell you about yourself. (Pause for one minute.)

After listening to your friend, you are allowed to ask a question that you wish to have answered about yourself. You can ask anything you want. You listen closely to the answer. (Pause.) Once you have your answer, your friend tells you that you can return here to the cave at anytime, that you are always welcome here. Your friend tells you that he or she will always be there to help you with anything that you need. You thank your friend, stand up, and calmly walk out of the cave. Then you walk back down the hill, over the bridge and once again look at your reflection in the water. You feel calm and relaxed and confident as you walk on the path, out of the forest and into a bright clearing. (Pause.) Now you become aware of the classroom and of sitting in your chair fully present. You become aware of your breathing and slowly open your eyes.

Extension: Have your students draw or write about their experience. Make sure you distribute the materials before beginning the narration.

Envisioneering Experience #2: My Positive Self

Goal: Students will determine and choose appropriate life ambitions, understanding that a positive self-image is desirable.

Time: 20 minutes (This activity will take longer if the extension activity is utilized.)

Setting: Classroom

Materials: None, unless your students complete a drawing of the experience. For the drawing, construction paper, crayons or markers will be needed.

Procedure: Have your students become relaxed and comfortable in their chairs. Make sure you have them concentrate on their breathing and then narrate the following:

Imagine yourself stepping into a marble tunnel that has white light overhead. The light in this tunnel gives off a very good energy and you feel energized now that you are in the tunnel. (Pause.) As you begin walking through the tunnel you pass through a warm water shower. You become dripping wet and very clean. (Pause.) Then a strong warm wind blows, and you and your clothes become dry. You step out of the tunnel of light onto a platform where it is very open. At the edge of the platform you notice that there are twenty-one steps going down to a door. Count backwards with me as you slowly walk down the stairs to the door. With each and every step let yourself become more and more relaxed. (Count slowly and softly with the students from 21 down to 0.) Now that you have come to the bottom of the stairs, open the door and walk into your own private room. This is your personal room so you can put anything into it you want–chairs, toys, stuffed animals, anything. Create anything you want to see in that room. (Pause.) Now you sit down into a large leather swivel chair. This is a very special chair. This chair has several controls on one of the armrests. One of the controls is hooked up to a large movie screen right in front of you. As you touch that control all of a sudden the movie screen in front of you lights up. The picture comes to focus and you notice that it is a picture of you in the future. You also notice that when you think about it, anything you want to have or become shows on the screen. You know that whatever you see on the screen will also become a part of your real life. (Pause.) When you see yourself on the screen as you would like to become, you press the second control on the armrest and a circle of white light goes around the screen. (Slight pause.) Then you press a third control and as you do, both the rim of white light and the screen begin to fade away into space. As the screen and white light begin to fade away, you are confident that you will have and become all that you have imagined. (Pause.) See yourself leaving your comfortable room, walking out, and counting the twenty-one steps as you climb back up. As you go back to the platform tell yourself that you will remember everything in your secret room and you will become all that you dream of. (Pause.)

Now slowly become aware of your breathing again, feel the cool air come through your nostrils and the warm air leave your mouth. You become aware of the room and slowly open your eyes feeling alert and terrific.

Extension: Before narrating this envisioneering experience pass out pieces of construction paper and crayons or markers so that when you have completed the narration your students can start right away on drawing what they experienced. Passing the papers out beforehand will allow the students to remain quiet and calm as they commence drawing.

Journal Writing for Promoting Competence

To feel competent, children must be aware of their strengths and weaknesses, have knowledge of their likes and dislikes, and be aware of their accomplishments. Students who are competent also know how to turn their mistakes into opportunities for learning. The following sentence stems are designed to help students become more aware of their competence.

- I am best at . . .

- I do these things very well . . .

- When I make a mistake . . .

- It's easy for me to . . .

- I want to be better at . . .

- I know all about . . .

- At home I know I can . . .

- If I were a bigger person, I could . . .

- If I were the boss, I would . . .

- My favorite thing to do at home on a Saturday is . . .

- If I don't give up, I can . . .

- Something I don't do very well is . . .

- When I try something new, I like to . . .

- When I do something wrong, I can . . .

- My favorite thing to do in school is . . .

- My friends and I like to play . . .

- Other people help me to . . .

- The best part about learning is . . .

- I am very brave when . . .

- I have the right to . . .

- The best thing I ever did was . . .

- When I try new things, I feel . . .

- I want to know about . . .

- I try hard to . . .

- I can . . .

- The hardest thing for me to do is . . .

- My teacher lets me . . .

- When I get older I'll be able to . . .

- I feel happy when . . .

- If I can't do something right the first time, I can . . .

- I don't like to . . .

- The easiest thing for me to do is . . .

- I get scared when I have to . . .

- One thing I am really good at is . . .

- Today I learned how to . . .

- I can help other people to . . .

- It was hard for me to do, but I was able to . . .

- It is becoming easier and easier to . . .

- I am responsible for . . .

- I choose to . . .

GA1501

Interdisciplinary Activities

Earth Science

Clouds

Goal: Students will understand that moisture in the air takes many forms and that clouds have characteristics by which they can be described and classified.

Time: Several days

Setting: Classroom, library, outside under the sky

Materials: Encyclopedias, tagboard, markers, black construction paper, cotton balls

Procedure: In the journey across the Atlantic, James and the Giant Peach encounter the scarey Cloud Men. Due to the obnoxious Centipede, the Cloud Men become angry and start throwing hailstones. What are these things called clouds? What are they made of? How many different types of clouds are there? How do clouds get up in the sky? What exactly are hailstones? What is thunder? What is lightning? You can be sure that asking these questions will arouse your students' curiosity. And once you have their interest, a lesson will surely result. Now the research begins! Have your students write reports, draw pictures, make posters, or observe clouds up in the sky. Go outside and have students discuss what forms or shapes they see in the sky. Check the newspaper for weather forecasts or have them watch the news for homework. Make sure they pay attention to the satellite photos of cloud cover throughout the country. Glue cotton balls to black construction paper to make models of the different types of clouds (make sure they draw the flying peach somewhere on the paper). For some clouds the cotton balls will be bunched up; for other clouds the cotton balls will be stretched out. Here are some cloud facts.

Major Types	Description
Cirrus:	White and feathery, high in the sky
Cumulus:	Puffy with flat bottoms, low in the sky
Stratus:	Wide gray blankets, low in the sky (drizzle or snow flurries)

Hailstones are chunks of ice that fall during thunderstorms. They are formed when tiny particles of dust and ice collide with cold water droplets.

Social Science

Coming to America

Goal: Students will understand that the early visitors coming to this country seeking freedom and economic opportunity had to meet immigration standards.

Time: Several days

Setting: Classroom

Materials: Paper, tagboard, markers, book-making materials

Procedure: James and all the creatures traveling on the peach were visitors to the United States. The United States is a nation peopled by visitors, called immigrants, from all over the world. In New York Harbor are both Liberty and Ellis Island. On Liberty Island stands the great monument, The Statue of Liberty. Given to the United States by France, this statue was constructed by the French sculptor, Bartholdi. The highest point of this great structure is the torch, a beacon of light, intended to be a symbol of enlightenment, truth, freedom, and liberty.

The Statue of Liberty looks directly toward the open water of New York Harbor, offering an invitation to immigrant travelers arriving in America. The most famous phrase from the poem on the base of the statue states, "Give me your tired, your poor, your huddled masses yearning to breathe free." For millions of immigrants, Liberty symbolized hope–hope that a new and better way of life could be found in America. However, the immigration center of Ellis Island provided the harsh reality of immigration laws for newcomers desiring to become American citizens. From 1892 to 1932 more than twelve million people from all over the world traveled to tiny Ellis Island. Imagine what it would have been like if James and all the creatures had to pass through Ellis Island. Would the laws have allowed all of them to stay in the United States? Would they have had to go home? After researching more about the statue and the immigration center, invite your students to write a story about what it would have been like if our travelers had to visit Ellis Island. Would their hopes of a better way of life have been denied? When completed, discuss how James and the creatures made America their "Land of Opportunity." Have your students write a story entitled "My Land of Opportunity" to explain what they plan to do with their future in the United States of America. Finally, ask your students who would like to construct a poster of the Statue of Liberty, and make sure they include the famous poem by Emma Lazarus which is inscribed on the statue's base.

Industrial Arts

The Empire State Building

Goal: Students will be able to demonstrate proper cooperative skills and sequences needed to construct a project.

Time: One and one-half hours

Setting: Classroom

Materials: Paper, pencils, 500-600 straws, 5 or 6 boxes of pins

Procedure: In *James and the Giant Peach*, after the peach and crew crossed the Atlantic Ocean, the giant fruit finally fell and landed on the pinnacle of the Empire State Building. Reality or fantasy? When it was built and opened on May 1, 1931, the Empire State Building was the biggest and highest building in the entire world. The architect, Frederick Lamb, sketched plans four times for the building before construction commenced, and in the twenty-five weeks it took to construct the building, fourteen men lost their lives. Hopefully, when your students construct their buildings it won't take so long, or be so dangerous. The materials each group of five or six students will be given are 100 straws and a box of pins. Getting stuck with a pin will probably be the most dangerous aspect of this project! Your mission, should you accept it, will be to have your student groups compete in the design and construction of the tallest building for your entire classroom. They can use the 100 straws and pins in any way they wish, and like the construction of the Empire State Building, there will be a time limit. If plans are to be drawn, an hour is usually sufficient. Try to guess how many problem-solving skills will be needed for this cooperative effort!

GA1501

Extra, Extra, Read All About It!

James and the Giant Peach make the newspaper. Write a headline and story. Then draw a picture of the adventure.

Write the headline.

GA1501

Decisions, Decisions

James had some pretty hard decisions to make. If you were James, what would you have done in those sticky situations? Be creative and write your decisions below; then draw a picture to illustrate your solution.

The sharks are thrashing about, trying to eat the peach! You must do something to save everyone. What would you do to save the peach?

_____

_____

_____

_____

Suddenly the silly Centipede fell off the peach. Will he be lost forever? What would you do to save Centipede?

_____

_____

_____

_____

The pesty Centipede yells and calls the Cloud Men names. They start throwing hailstones at the peach. How are you going to get out of this mess?

_____

_____

_____

_____

GA1501

What Would Have Happened?

Magic crystals? The old man said they would solve all of James' problems if he drank them right away. James would never be miserable again! Marvelous, fabulous, unbelievable things would happen if James drank the magic crystals. How would you write the story if James really did drink the magic crystals?

_____

_____

_____

_____

_____

_____

_____

_____

_____

Draw a picture to go along with your story.

GA1501

End of the Journey

The great journey on the giant peach across the vast ocean finally came to an end. But our adventurers lived on. And each of them became very successful and rich in America. Many people have come to America thinking of it as "The Land of Opportunity." How did each of our characters become successful in America?

The Centipede became _____

_____

The Earthworm became _____

_____

The Silkworm and Miss Spider became _____

_____

The Glow-worm became _____

_____

The Old-Green Grasshopper became _____

_____

The Ladybug became _____

_____

And James Henry Trotter himself became _____

_____

Dreams Do Come True

After all their struggles and adventures everyone who traveled on the peach across the ocean became successful in America. Each of them learned a great deal on the journey. They learned that life is a journey and each of us has the power to make our dreams come true. What about you? What do you dream of becoming? In the space below draw a picture of your life as you would most like it to be. Then write a paragraph describing your successful life. What kind of career will you have? Who will be with you? Where will you live?

_____

_____

_____

_____

_____

_____

_____

_____

GA1501

Victory Log

One of the first steps to becoming a winner is remembering all the good things you have done. Think about all the great things you have done so far. When you were just a little kid you learned how to walk. When you were just a little kid you learned how to talk. Those are big things! It may not seem like it now but at the time you did them, they were. Now is the time to write down ten big things that you have done in your life.

Write down your strengths and achievements.

1. _____
2. _____
3. _____
4. _____
5. _____
6. _____
7. _____
8. _____
9. _____
10. _____

"I have learned that success is to be measured not so much by the position that one has reached in life as by the obstacles which he has overcome while trying to succeed."
— *Booker T. Washington*

Superstar Students

Below you will find six pieces to a puzzle. These pieces form a perfect star when put together correctly. First follow the directions below to make the pieces personal. Next cut the pieces out and put them together to make a star. Then use a piece of construction paper and glue the pieces together and trim around the star shape. Finally have your teacher hang up your star somewhere in the classroom. You're the Superstar Student.

On   draw a picture of yourself and write your name.

On   use three words to explain what kind of person you are.

On   list three things you like to do.

On   list what you think is "cool" about yourself.

On   write what your friends like about you.

On   write your goal for the future.

GA1501

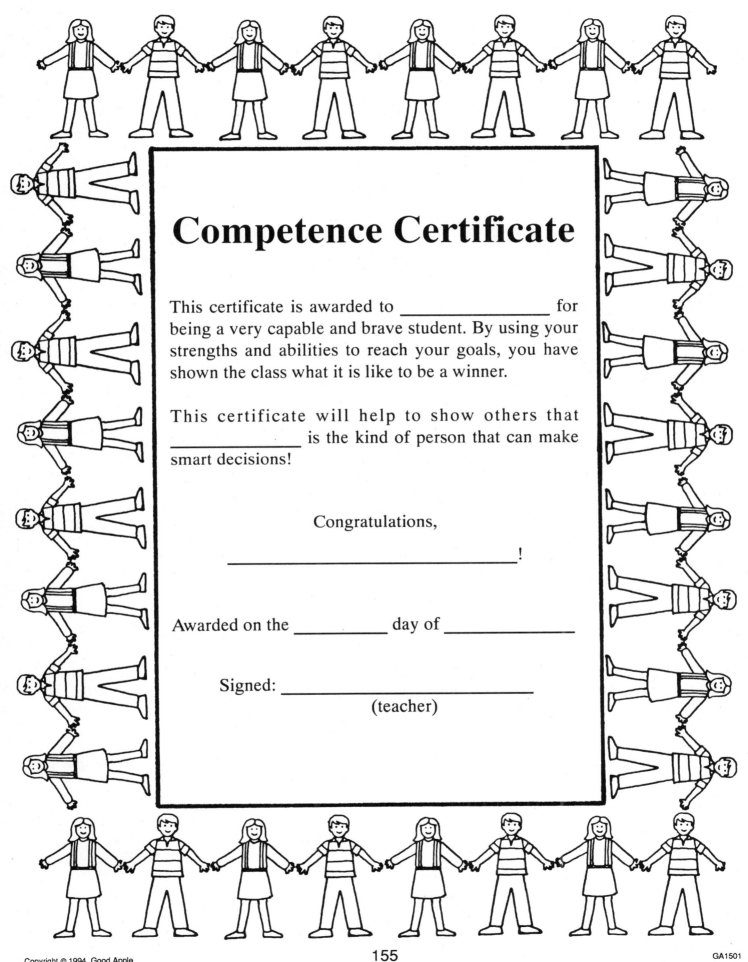

Competence Certificate

This certificate is awarded to _____ for being a very capable and brave student. By using your strengths and abilities to reach your goals, you have shown the class what it is like to be a winner.

This certificate will help to show others that _____ is the kind of person that can make smart decisions!

Congratulations,

_____!

Awarded on the _____ day of _____

Signed: _____
(teacher)

155

GA1501

Developing Your Own Thematic Units

"The man who does not read good books has no advantage over the man who can't read them."
– Mark Twain

What Is Theme Teaching?

A theme is a subject of discourse, topic, issue, problem, experience, or "big idea." Thematic units are integrated long-term learning experiences around which other ideas, concepts, and skills are clustered and integrated. Thematic units are meant to be literature-based, enriched, and extended. A thematic unit focuses on learning, making sure that it has function, meaning, and purpose. It offers the teacher an opportunity to establish an environment that enhances and encourages process learning. Thematic units allow children to experience connections between the subject or topic and their own world. When children are presented with a theme or topic that has personal meaning and with ideas and activities that they can use in their everyday world, they acquire knowledge and understanding the natural way, motivated by the curiosity and desire to grow.

So, what does all this mean? Well, when you develop a thematic unit, first you pick a big idea, a theme like trust. Then you search for a core literature book that fits, one that will support that theme. When you've done that, then you try to figure out ways to integrate as many different subject areas or disciplines around that theme as possible. You think to yourself, "Let's see . . . how can I get social science, science, health, multicultural education, industrial technology, physical education, music, visual arts, and math to support this theme of trust?" But wait, because you're not done yet. After you do that then you'll need to think of what specific concepts and skills from each of the subject areas you're going to teach. Then you have to think of the activities and lessons you will use to teach those concepts and skills. That seems like a lot of work, doesn't it? Yes, it is! But it's worth it because the kids love it and they learn from it. That's what thematic teaching is all about.

Thematic Doctrines

Let's cover the basic doctrines of thematic teaching before getting into the actual development of thematic units. When a teacher begins the development of an effective thematic unit, these things must be kept in mind.

1. When activities and ideas are integrated and interrelated as they are in life, children learn best. Children never learn in time blocks at home or in real life, so why should they at school?

2. Thematic units gather disciplines or subject areas around a central idea. You're constantly asking yourself, "How can I get math, science, or whatever subject area to fit into this theme?" Some subjects are easy to fit; others can be a bear to get in. Don't worry about trying to get them all in—nobody can. If you can't, then teach them in isolation. That's part of the game!

3. Thematic teaching emphasizes the use of processes for constructing meaning, solving problems, and discovering relationships. A process is a systematic series of actions directed toward some end. The end–meaning and understanding. What sort of processes? You know, writing processes–stuff like that.

4. The teacher and students are in charge of the curriculum. Encourage students to take on more responsibility for determining the learning direction of your thematic units. In a whole language program activities are meant to be learner-centered and meaningful to the student. By allowing a student to make choices and own some part of the curriculum, he or she will become more involved and motivated.

5. Students are allowed to work at their appropriate developmental levels and are encouraged to explore their interests. Sometimes this can be the greatest gift you can give to students–letting them be themselves.

6. Students become engaged in dynamic, experiential learning. The classroom is a busy place. Kids are interacting and involved; projects are in the process of being completed; desks are strewn all over the place. Real learning is going on.

A Word About Interdisciplinary Instruction

Thematic units require teachers to organize several subject areas together in order to parallel the kinds of problems encountered in real life. This interdisciplinary instruction applies more than one discipline to examine the central theme, issue, problem, topic, or experience. However, the teacher should be aware that students cannot fully benefit from interdisciplinary studies until they have a solid grounding in each of the individual disciplines that is attempting to be bridged. Therefore, thematic units should focus on natural cross-disciplinary or multidisciplinary relationships. In other words, the connection or bridge should come easily and be readily recognizable.

Into, Through, and Beyond

When developing a thematic unit the first objective to consider is how to get into, or start, the unit. Teachers want to be thinking, "What is going to create interest for the learner?" "How can I begin to motivate the students to want to become involved with this theme?" "How can I relate what we are about to do to their everyday world?" Asking questions about the theme itself while recording student responses is a good way to get started. Talking about a personal experience that directly relates to the theme and then asking students to share similar experiences is another way. Maybe you can think of an activity to introduce that relates to the theme. Some activity variations might include songs, poems, artwork, games, or maybe there is a short story or picture book that you could read that will help to introduce the theme.

Once you are into the theme the next step is to read about the theme. At this time the class is reading through their core literature book. An abundance of activities should be emanating from the book itself. Some of the activities have been developed by you, and other activities have spawned from student interest. As many subject areas as possible are being worked into the process of relating to and understanding the theme. The class is working and interacting together, in groups and individually. Listening, speaking, reading, writing, and moving activities are taking place. Everybody is busy relating to the theme.

To go beyond the theme, it is a good idea to culminate with a whole class project that will allow the children to apply all the knowledge gleaned from the theme. Perhaps your whole class project has been developing throughout the learning of the theme. Try to have the project relate, as much as possible, to the core literature book that was used. And finally, include a component in your teaching of the theme that includes the parents at home. It would be nice to involve those at home to reinforce the learning in school.

The Five-Step Method for Developing Thematic Units

All of this theme teaching seems pretty hard, but developing a thematic unit is relatively simple once you know how. I previously explained how to develop a thematic unit, but to make it easier to understand I've broken down the process into five steps. Here they are.

1. Select a theme and core literature book.
2. Identify teacher and student objectives related to the theme.
3. Determine the specific skills to be addressed.
4. Find resources.
5. Choose activities.

Step 1: Select a theme and core literature book.

A theme is a big idea around which other ideas or concepts may be gathered and integrated. When selecting themes, consideration is given to the following criteria:

1. The theme must be a subject of discourse, topic, issue, problem, or experience–not an object such as an apple.
2. The theme must be of interest to you and your students.
3. The theme must be large enough so that it can be divided into smaller "subthemes" that can be related to the larger theme.
4. The theme must not be geographically or historically limiting.
5. The theme must be comprehensive enough to break down artificial barriers between subjects and also those barriers between school and the "real world."

After selecting the theme then find a core literature book appropriate for your grade level that will support that particular theme. Look around, read a few books, and pick one that you like and one that you think the kids will like. A good book, when worked with in a whole language approach will, with the teacher's help, provide opportunities to attend to children's cognitive, affective, and psychomotor domains. There are three categories of literature to be used in a thematic unit.

a. Core literature is used as the base for directed and in-depth instruction during the language arts time period. This selection specifically addresses the instructional theme being explored in the unit. Each student should have a copy of the book in his or her first language and adequate access to cultural adaptations of the same core literature selection.

b. Extended literature includes those books suggested or assigned by the teacher for individual or small group work. These books support and supplement the core literature selection of the unit. These selections are appropriately used for thematic research and development.

GA1501

c. Recreational literature is those books with universal appeal supplied by the teacher to be read or heard for pleasure and because the student has an interest in the subject, style, author, or illustrator. Book boxes can be provided with enough selections provided to keep students interested in the theme.

Step 2: Identify teacher and student objectives related to the theme.

The second step consists of breaking the theme into smaller parts and identifying the reasons why this theme is an important one to explore. Articulating these objectives will provide direction for the theme and subsequent activities. They are the large learning outcomes that you intend as a result of your theme study.

Step 3: Determine the specific skills to be addressed.

You should also articulate those instructional goals you will be targeting for each academic subject area. Goals should be drawn from as many subject areas as possible when developing your thematic unit. Referring to the subject areas listed in your district or state curriculum guide will help you identify key concepts for your grade level. In the units outlined in this book, you will find these subject goals listed at the beginning of each activity.

Step 4: Find resources.

Materials that you choose must be focused enough to provide structure for an integrated curriculum. As you assemble materials, ask yourself, "If I were to show all these materials to other teachers or to my students, would they be able to figure out the theme?"

Collect a variety of materials from many resources—magazines, newspapers, encyclopedias, trade books, maps, music, etc. These materials should come from a variety of subject areas and be able to interrelate around the theme. As students interact with materials from different sources and from different subject areas, they will develop a deeper understanding of the theme.

Step 5: Choose activities.

At this step, activities which relate directly to the identified concepts and skills are compiled from the content areas. The activities should be conceptually related to one another so students will continue to build on their background knowledge as they create meaning.

The following questions should be answered affirmatively when developing activities for the theme.

a. Are the activities conceptually linked to the theme?

b. Do the activities come from a variety of subject areas (literature, health, social science, physical education, etc.)?

c. Are the activities presented giving students the opportunity to repeatedly encounter a set of interrelated meanings throughout the theme unit?

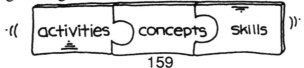

d. Are the activities giving consideration to how the students can use their prior knowledge to make meaning of the current activity?

e. What new knowledge will the students obtain from this experience which can be used as a base for future activities?

Finally, all activities and materials in the theme unit should provide students with opportunities for independent learning, problem solving, and risk taking.

When you decide to turn your classroom into a "whole language classroom" you begin to realize that it takes time to change teaching methods. It takes time to become comfortable with new ways of teaching. Some experts say that it takes from two to five years to become a true "whole language teacher." Hopefully this five-step method for developing thematic units will make the transition a little easier.

The two-page form provided will help you to develop your own thematic units. It is important to develop your own thematic units and not just rely on reproducible material for use in your own classroom–that is not true whole language teaching. In order to be able to really become a whole language teacher one must experience or "do" the process of comprising a thematic unit and incorporating those practices in the classroom. After all, as I am sure we are all aware, this is how our students learn best–by "doing."

I hear, and I forget
I see, and I remember
I do, and I understand.

Chinese Proverb

GA1501

Thematic Unit Development Form

1. Theme: _____ Grade Level: _____

   Core Literature Book: _____

2. Objectives:

3. Skills:

4. Resources:

5. Activities:

Teacher Attitude

"Teachers affect eternity; they can never tell where their influence stops."
– Henry Adams

Learning = a Change in Behavior

Using a whole language approach for enhancing self-esteem may require many of us to change the way we are currently teaching in our classrooms. However, we want our students to learn and grow. And students learn and grow by improving their self-value which is accomplished by changing behavior–changing the way they think and feel about themselves. Psychological change is uncomfortable; it's downright scarey at times, even for teachers. But everyone wants to be a winner, and the one thing all winners remember is this: "Winners are those people who make a habit of doing the things others feel uncomfortable doing!" Winners are accustomed to stepping outside of their comfort zone, changing their behavior, learning and growing. Winners take risks toward improvement. When a person steps outside the comfort zone, he or she has more room. Winners like room, and they realize that the largest room in the world is the room for improvement. Whole language teaching is not easy, but I urge you to give it a try.

The Silent Curriculum

The relationship a teacher has with his or her students is known as "The Silent Curriculum." This silent curriculum is the context in which all student/teacher interactions transpire. It is our attitude that underlines all that we do in the classroom. There are three teacher attributes or attitudes that contribute to students becoming independent learners: (1) becoming real; (2) care, acceptance, and trust; (3) empathic understanding.

When we are genuine with our students we have no false fronts. Our inner thoughts and feelings match our outer expressions. The things we say, the way we say them, and how our body communicates are congruent. We become authentic or real. When we care enough to accept and recognize our students' right to have feelings, we notice that students become less defensive and begin to trust. When we have accurate empathic understanding, we can voice our knowledge and wisdom of the experienced feelings of the child. When all of these attributes are present from the teacher for the student, students will use the relationship for growth and change, and personal development will occur.

These three attributes will help us achieve our main goal in education, to produce independent, autonomous thinkers and learners. Remember, the focus of education is to liberate children, not domesticate them.

162

GA1501

Teacher Self-Evaluations

Constant and ongoing evaluation should be a part of every effective teacher's pedagogy. Questions that we ask of ourselves need to keep us on track and help us be aware of whether our own personal needs are being met. You're fooling yourself if you don't think that it's important to have your needs met in the classroom. Yes, your students' needs are of primary importance, but if you don't feel that your needs are being met, eventually your interaction and performance will reflect that deficiency. Take the time to ask yourself some simple and refreshing questions. Decide for yourself whether or not your time in the classroom is rewarding for you. And if it's not, then maybe you need to make some changes. If you don't, you may not be very effective for very long.

Ask yourself:
• Do I acknowledge and remember the things that I did that worked today?
• Do I ask questions that allow the children to do the most talking rather than me?
• Do I bring much laughter and happiness into the classroom?
• Do I have to be right all the time?
• Do I acknowledge my strengths consistently?
• Do I provide ways to recognize progress in the classroom?
• Do I acknowledge that my mistakes are useful and something to be learned from?
• Do I model purposeful and inquisitive behavior in my classroom?
• Do I enjoy my time in the classroom with the children?
• Do I express my feelings adequately and appropriately?
• Do I think positively of myself in the classroom?
• Do I reward myself for a job well done?

Teacher Self-Esteem

Remember the self-esteem-building tools that we have to enhance our students' self-esteem? Well, there is one tool that I haven't mentioned until now, and that tool is the most important tool of the classroom. The teacher is the primary "tool" of any classroom. Your students learn more from your personhood than they do from anything else presented to them in that classroom. You are the model, the message of that classroom. Your students watch everything you say and do; they learn from you.

If you have carefully considered addressing the issue of self-esteem in your classroom, I'm sure you have sensed that the material on children's self-esteem applies to adults as well. Self-esteem issues have universal application, and it would be dangerous if we didn't consider teachers' self-esteem as part of the equation in enhancing student self-esteem.

I've heard the expression, "You can't give something away that you yourself don't have." Personally I have given consideration to this expression when thinking about what I have to give to the children in my classroom. I ask myself questions like, "Are my actions creating problems for the children?" "I wonder if I said the right thing to Dominique to help motivate her?" "Are my words empowering the children or are they creating self-doubt?" And what I have found is that when I recall the five steps in the process of enhancing self-esteem (trust, community, self-awareness, purpose, and competence) and how I begin to develop each step into a self-esteem thematic unit, I find that I teach those steps best that I have learned the best for myself.

GA1501

• To the level that you are able to trust in your classroom, the students will feel secure.

• To the level that you feel a sense of community, the students will feel accepted.

• To the level that you are self-aware, the students will have an identity.

• To the level that you have purpose, the students will be motivated.

• And to the level that you are competent, the students will feel like winners in your classroom.

Affirming Declarations for the Educator

Sometimes teachers need a little boost to get the day going. Our day can get a little difficult. And all too often there is no one there to help bring us up. That's when we can use affirming declarations to do it ourselves. Here are a few for us teachers and a little space to create your own.

1. I teach as I choose to, and as a result I enjoy my increased effectiveness.

2. I am loving and supportive to all my students, inspiring them to be all that they can be.

3. I respond effortlessly to every classroom situation.

4. I am calmly teaching with creativity and zest.

5. I trust myself as I work at my own speed.

6. I am a powerful and radiant teacher filled with joy and love.

7. I am joyfully loving and giving to myself and others.

8. I am creatively enhancing the spirit of love within myself and my students.

Your turn.

1. _____

2. _____

3. _____

4. _____

5. _____

6. _____

7. _____

8. _____

GA1501

Teacher Goal Work Sheet

If we are to teach goal-setting strategies and techniques, we must first know how to set our own goals. Here is an opportunity for the teacher to go through the goal-setting process for his or her classroom. A teacher must know where he or she wants to take students. If you're not sure where you're going, you're liable to end up someplace else!

Describe what your classroom climate is like right now.

_____

_____

_____

Describe the ideal image of what your classroom would look, feel, and sound like.

_____

_____

_____

List the reasons why you would like your classroom climate to look, feel, and sound this way.

_____

_____

_____

Write your goals. (Check subsequent pages for examples.)

My classroom will _____

by _____

I will_____

by _____

I will_____

by _____

I will_____

by _____

GA1501

Identify the resources you will use to accomplish your goals.

_____

_____

_____

Develop your plan. Use an intelligent sense of logical progression. Start with your ultimate outcome and work backwards until you can find something that you can do today to support your goals.

5. _____

4. _____

3. _____

2. _____

1. _____

Now . . . TAKE ACTION!
This information must get up off the paper and actually
be put to practice in your classroom to be of any good.
Just do it!

"Whatever you can do or dream, you can begin. Boldness has genius, power, and magic in it."
– Goethe

The last step is to acknowledge yourself when you actually accomplish your goal. Celebrate if you made it! Go out and treat yourself; maybe you'll want to include the students too! Teachers actually need to see that they have reached specific goals in the classroom. All too often it is very difficult to see the results of our work. Setting goals and achieving them is one way teachers become rewarded and intrinsically motivated.

Teacher Goal Examples

Maybe you would like to use one of the goals listed here as your own. If not, personalize a goal to fit your needs.

I will use two self-esteem-building experiential activities per week, throughout the current school year.

I will develop a thematic unit to support the self-esteem theme of trust using a core literature book appropriate for my grade level as a resource.

I will pick one child per day to nourish with at least ten praisings.

I will teach goal-setting strategies to the children in my classroom by the end of this week.

I will construct a Super Student of the Week bulletin board to be used throughout the year by Friday, September 1.

I will make a conscious effort to catch my students doing something right, expressing more positive statements throughout the day.

I will involve the class in two cooperative activities every week for the next four weeks.

Teachers, Why Are We Here?

Don't you think it's really great being a teacher? Think of all the stimulating, challenging, fun and loving things teachers get to do! If you don't agree with these thoughts, it may be that you're in the wrong profession. Teaching is a profession, but more than that, teaching is a vocation.

Albert Einstein said when thinking about the purpose of man's existence, "Strange is our situation here upon earth. Each of us comes for a short visit, not knowing why, but sometimes seeming to divine a purpose."

For some, teaching is a calling and, if willing, a divine calling. Honestly, teaching is what you make of it. You create your own reality in that classroom regardless of all the administrative and social shortcomings surrounding you. You own that classroom. You're in that room, with those children, six or more hours a day. You are the leader of that classroom and you have to ask yourself, "What kind of experience do I wish to create in my classroom?" The teacher is the thermostat of that room, not the thermometer. You control the environment in that room and ultimately, you make the decision as to exactly what happens in that classroom, no one else.

So, what are you teaching in that room? Are you teaching curriculum or are you teaching children? Why did you really become a teacher? Was it to teach diphthongs and digraphs, or subject-verb agreement? I think not. What turns you on the most about teaching? What is your passion? What is the reason you became a teacher in the first place? My guess is that your deciding to become a teacher was not something that was just a fluke. Why did you become a teacher?

Schools and school districts all have mission statements–so should teachers. To teach means to guide and direct. So unless you have a mission or purpose of your own, how are you going to guide and direct your students? Teachers must have a purpose of their own!

What's a Purpose?

- Your purpose is the reason why you exist.
- Your purpose guides you, gives you meaning and direction.
- Your purpose remains constant for life and it is fulfilled in each moment.
- Your purpose is something that brings you so much satisfaction and pleasure that you are willing to devote your whole life to it.
- Your purpose provides focus for your activities and makes the process of coming to decisions much easier.

When you are aware of your life's purpose you waste less energy and you are more centered. You have a certain power and confidence that no one can take away from you. One of the most important actions you can take is to . . .

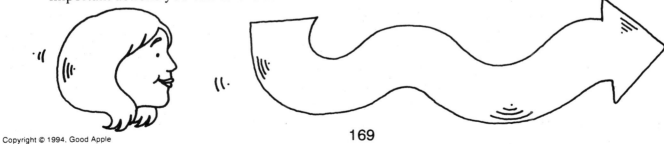

GA1501

Determine Your Purpose!

A. List your most prized qualities: things you appreciate in yourself, qualities you enjoy using.

Examples: Enthusiasm, creativity, humor, friendliness, energy, caring, power, strength.

1. _____   2. _____

3. _____   4. _____

B. List four ways you enjoy expressing your qualities when interacting with others.

Examples: Instructing, teaching, exploring, writing, supporting, playing, giving, working.

1. _____   2. _____

3. _____   4. _____

C. Write a brief statement of your vision of a perfect world. What does it look like? How is everyone interacting?

Example: Healthy, physically fit people becoming all they are capable of and living within a clean, supportive, peaceful environment.

Combine the three prior subdivisions (A, B, and C) in a single statement.

My purpose is to use my_____(A)

and my _____(A)

by _____(B)

and _____(B)

so that _____

_____

_____(C)

GA1501

Do We Make a Difference?

Teachers, we work hard, really hard! And sometimes we wonder if all our efforts are making a difference. Sometimes the obstacles in front of us seem insurmountable. At times progress begins to feel slow in the classroom. Then we realize that the general public thinks we're doing a poor job, administrators often don't support us, sometimes parents don't thank us, budget cuts confront us, and then the pay cuts come. That's when we begin to wonder why we're in this profession.

Then something wonderful happens. A girl in your classroom starts to take responsibility for her learning, and she reads much more than she ever was able to before. The class starts working together beautifully on a special project. Everyone is helping one another and faces are smiling. You take a step back to watch what's happening knowing that you helped to create this. A tear comes to your eye, and you have to look away because you don't want the children to see you getting too emotional. Then you go home on cloud nine for the rest of the evening.

Then it's back to work the next day, and unfortunately at times things begin to look grim all over again. Sometimes it's hard to tell if the children are learning. You ask yourself, "Is anything I'm doing making a difference?" It begins to feel as if the good times are too few and far between. That's when we begin to question ourselves and our efforts all over again. It's at times like those when I like to remember this story that I believe illustrates the significance teachers have in the lives of their students.

An old man happened to be walking along the beach one morning at dawn when he noticed a most peculiar sight. Ahead of him on the beach he observed a young boy surrounded by thousands of starfish. The old man gazed in wonder as the young boy again and again picked up a small starfish and threw it into the water. Finally, the old man approached the boy and asked him why he spent so much energy doing what seemed to be such a waste of time. The little boy explained that the stranded starfish would soon die if left until the hot morning sun. The old man replied, "Yeah, but there must be thousands of miles of beach and millions of starfish. How can your efforts make a difference?" The young boy looked down at the small starfish on the sand, bent over, picked it up, and tossed it to safety into the ocean and said, "It made a difference to that one."

It may not seem like it at times but, teachers, we really do make a difference. And even if it's just one student that we're touching the life of, the effort is well worth it.

Keep up the good work!

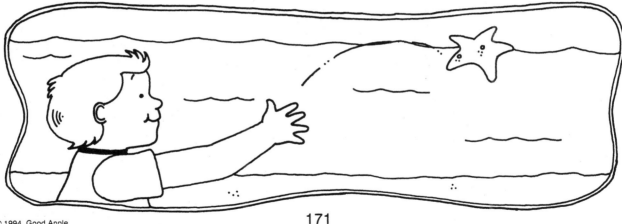

GA1501

Bibliography

Banathy, B.H. *Systems Design of Education: A Journey to Create the Future.* Englewood Cliffs, NJ: Educational Technology Publications, 1991.

Blanchard, K., and S. Johnson. *The One Minute Manager.* New York, NY: William Morrow and Co. Inc., 1982.

Borba, Dr. Michele. *Esteem Builders: A K-8 Curriculum for Improving Student Achievement, Behavior and School Climate.* Rolling Hills Estates, CA: Jalmar Press, 1989.

Branden, Nathaniel. *The Psychology of Self-Esteem.* Los Angeles, CA: Nash Publishing Corp., 1971.

Canfield, Jack. *Self-Esteem in the Classroom: A Curriculum Guide.* Pacific Palisades, CA: Self-Esteem Seminars, 1986.

Coopersmith, Stanley. *The Antecedents of Self-Esteem.* San Francisco, CA: W.H. Freedman and Company, 1967.

Dahl, Roald. *James and the Giant Peach.* New York, NY: Knopf, 1961.

Devencenzi, Jayne, and Sue Pendergast. *Belonging: A Guide for Group Facilitators.* San Luis Obispo, CA: Belonging, 1988.

Gilroy, Pamela. *Discovery in Motion: Movement Exploration for Problem Solving and Self-Concept.* Tucson, AZ: Communication Skill Builders, 1989.

Ledwig, Mark. "There's No One Like Me." Los Angeles, CA: Elementary Rock and Roll, 1990.

Los Angeles Unified School District, Office of Elementary Instruction. *Elementary School Course of Study, Publication No. EC-606-1990.*

Murdock, Maureen. *Spinning Inward: Using Guided Imagery with Children for Learning, Creativity and Relaxation.* Boston, MA: Shambhala Publications, Inc., 1987.

New Games Foundation, *The New Games Book.* New York, NY: Headlands Press, Inc., 1976.

Orlick, Terry. *The Cooperative Sports and Games Book: Challenge Without Competition.* New York, NY: Pantheon Books, 1978.

Piper, Watty. *The Little Engine That Could.* New York, NY: Platt & Munk, Co. 1990.

Robbins, Anthony. *Awaken the Giant Within.* New York, NY: Summit Books, Inc.

Seuss, Dr. *Oh, the Places You'll Go!* New York, NY: Random House, 1990.

Toward a State of Esteem: The Final Report of the California Task Force to Promote Self-Esteem and Personal and Social Responsibility. Sacramento, CA: California State Department of Education, 1990.

White, E.B. *Charlotte's Web.* New York, NY: HarperCollins, 1952.

White, M., and D. Epston. *Narrative Means to Theraputic Ends.* New York, NY: W.W. Norton & Company, Inc., 1990.

Williams, Margery. *The Velveteen Rabbit.* New York, NY: Henry Holt and Co., 1983.

Yashima, Taro. *Crow Boy.* New York, NY: Puffin Books, 1976.

GA1501